grief
CLIMB TOWARD UNDERSTANDING

grief
CLIMB TOWARD UNDERSTANDING

*Self–help when
you are struggling*

*Includes checklists
of what you can do*

By Phyllis Davies

Illustrations by Itoko Maeno

A Lyle Stuart Book
Published by Carol Communications

A Lyle Stuart Book
Published by Carol Communications

Editorial Offices
600 Madison Avenue
New York, NY 10022

Sales & Distribution Offices
120 Enterprise Avenue
Secaucus, NJ 07094

In Canada: Musson Book Company
A division of General Publishing Co. Limited
Don Mills, Ontario

Manufactured in the United States of America

ISBN 0-8184-0490-6

To Bill and Dawna

CONTENTS

PREFACE

On August 24, 1984, Derek, our thirteen-year-old son, was killed in a midair plane collision.

By January 1985, I felt like a volcano ready to explode. I was caught in the magma of memories swirling around me. I could no longer see the individual parts. These memories of him completely occupied my mind: the ring he gave me, his rope, dancing with him, music, the children playing together, working together on the farm, even the angels. Love for life and family is equaled by depth of sorrow. It was in my sorrow that I began to write. My thoughts formed in free verse.

After I had completed much of the writing, I received the book *The Courage to Grieve*, by Judy Tatelbaum. As I turned the pages, it was a replay of the lessons that had been instrumental in helping me develop my deepest understandings about life. Most importantly, in her book she asked me if I was ready, then encouraged me through that step of resolution.

This collection has been sequenced using the categories that Judy's book suggested. Her book helped me organize my concepts of the phases of grief and understand my growth process. These writings naturally fell into the same five categories, which I interpret metaphorically as five summits. The illustrations reflect this metaphor.

My husband Bill, our teen-age daughter Dawna and I have had strongly contrasting grief experiences. I cannot write of theirs, they cannot write of mine. We found we had known Derek from different perspectives, although we had each been close to him. We each had a unique partnership with him, along with being on a family team. Struggling through this grief, both together and alone, has increased my love and admiration for Bill and Dawna.

When years ago we had a stillborn baby, I simply closed off those awful memories; I couldn't cope with them and didn't know help was available. Then while I was in the middle of my grief for Derek, I suddenly discovered the unfinished grief for our other son.

I have found it is important to understand that grief comes into life in many different forms. Death creates grief. It is not the only grief, although it is often the most devastating.

Living on a diversified small farm with animals, our family has experienced grief as an integral part of life. Especially when a pet dies or even as a farm animal is sold or dies, I have dealt with degrees of grief. I find I experience grief when a friend moves or when a divorce between friends occurs. I now realize grief is present even in life's happy moments, such as graduations, promotions and weddings, because these all require changes.

I have no illusions of literary excellence. I had written these pieces for myself. They helped my healing process and have often been helpful or encouraging to others struggling with the loss of a loved one.

You will find included with my writing two meaningful poems written by others.

The checklists and other information in the reference section are my response to coping with the decisions that need to be made during the grief process. They stand in harsh contrast to the poetry. Yet I feel they warrant inclusion as they too are part of my story.

Grief comes with life. Understanding there are five steps in grief made it possible for me to complete the grief process with time. As a result, I have found new purpose and joy in life.

I hope this collection will inspire you to begin to unlock your own hurt, anger, sorrow and joy on paper.

Phyllis Davies

P.S. Today, as this book goes to press, four and a half years after his death we received this note from some of his classmates.
   "We wanted you to know we remember Derek. He walked lightly and responsibly on this earth, all the years we went to school with him. The power of his gentle thoughtfulness and compentetence continues to walk beside us. He is listed in memory as a member of our San Luis Obispo High School Class of 1989."

WRITING AS A TOOL FOR HEALING

After Derek's death I needed to write down my memories, but I was afraid. All my life, attempts to write have been hampered by a learning disability that makes writing and reading difficult. An advertisement in the newspaper for a writing workshop caught my eye. Something, naggingly encouraged me to enroll. My grief experiences and memories unfolded onto paper through the ideas introduced in the suggested text, *Writing the Natural Way*, by Gabriele Rico. It helped me cut the chains of failure and criticism that had bound me since childhood.

The release from grief has been slow – two steps ahead, one back. At times the paper was so wet with tears it would tear as I wrote the next word, so I would start again on another sheet of paper. I tried to write about thoughts, experiences, feelings and flashbacks as they occurred.

The "clustering" process from Gabriele's book has been particularly helpful to me and for those in the writing group that meets twice a month at my office. We have continued to use the book as a guide for our writing.

Most of the pieces, in their original form, have been written to Derek. Upon finishing each writing, I have felt relief and pleasure, accompanied by another level of closeness to him. It feels much like sitting and talking, sharing thoughts with a very dear friend.

Writing has helped me enter fully into my sorrow. In doing so, I began to discover that there are gifts hidden in the grief experience. Although there has been great sorrow from Derek's death, there has been great joy in sharing and helping others with their own sorrow. It has helped me progress through grief to a release and peace. Most of the time, I now can remember Derek without crying inside or out.

Writing is a creative expression that has helped me keep my commitment to grow through the experiences I face in life and to live in the present rather than in the past.

CLIMB TOWARD UNDERSTANDING

628 or 624

No one
would tell
us anything.

Radio report.

A midair collision.
Wings West Flight 628.

11:17 a.m.

"Wings West 624 – 11:00"
was written in
my daily log.

All
phones
busy –
airlines,
airport.

Airport.
In person.
"I'm sorry;
we have no information."

Hospital
emergency room.
"No survivors from 628."

"But was there a 624 at 11:00?"

A flash of anger.

RED-HOT STEEL

branded

life
forever

BEFORE   624

     and

AFTER   628.

Hours passed.
Not knowing,
we waited,
prayed,
waited,
waited.

3:00.
Derek's
arrival time,
Reno Airport.

Phoned.
No answer.
Again,
busy signals.
Again,

Again,
finally
someone answered.

We asked,
"Would you
please page
Derek Davies?"

We waited

waited

waited.

Coldly said:
"No answer to the page."

So we waited,
waited.

After dark
the sheriff called.

"Your son's body
has been identified."

There had been no 624.

Only 628.

Derek is dead.

Derek is dead?
Waiting.
Waited.

What?

D E R E K

D E A D

Wait, what?
Derek, dead.

Derek . . .

No waiting.

Wait, I want to wait a minute more.

FIVE-SUMMIT JOURNEY

Suddenly
trapped,
tied in
aimless
struggle.

Lashed
by emotion,
unknown gales.

Slowly,
I began to see
what was happening to me,
to understand grief
as a process.

Mountains
loomed
ahead
above me
in a range
of strange-
named peaks.

SHOCK,
the first summit
in this mountain range,
caught me unprepared
for the grueling climb.

On the peak of
DISORDERED SUFFERING
the storms of memories
lashed, swirled
about me constantly.

NEW ORDER,
a third crag,
emerged from the fog.

PERSPECTIVE,
summit four,
revealed
understandings
never seen or felt before.

RESOLUTION,
a small knoll,
demands a courageous stroll,
as the sun sets into
the twilight of my grief.

The first
three summits
are exhausting,
inner-driven climbs
for all but those
who die of grief.

On that third peak
we stop,
rest, and ask,

"Why go on?"

Bewildered,
we look out across
the last two summits:
PERSPECTIVE
then
RESOLUTION.

On the peak
NEW ORDER,
life becomes
almost tolerable again.

Yet
we must
trudge on through
this mountain range.

How many die still crying?

Healing comes
in crossing
all five
summits.

Unresolved grief
saps,
sucks
all one has
to give to life.

Its cost
is beyond belief
for you, for me,
for our world –
all whose lives we touch.

No traditions urge us on.
Those celebrations,
milestone markers,
cheers of support
along the way.

The structure
and support
of tradition,
"luto,"
"the wake,"
"widow's weeds,"
the "mourning year,"
once guided us,
now lost,
as our culture
became a mix of many.

Bereavement differs greatly.

We now understand
grief as a process.

If it be
fifty years of grieving,
get up, go on,
cross the hill of **RESOLUTION.**

Join me.

Say
thank you,
grief.

I am who
I am today,
in part,
because
I have crossed
these five summits.

THIS BOOK

I'm standing here
looking back across
these peaks of grief,

along trod paths
worn through rock,
washed with tears
since time began.

For me,
it's been
a journey
of two years.

My hand drew this map.
It's here for you to use.

As I set it down,
just know
I'll walk this trail again
with you, if you wish.

It's an easier hike for me now
to cross this mountain range.
I know we'll be illumined
by the panorama of peace.

As we walk, we'll marvel
at what once went unnoticed.
You'll meet and grow to know
one of my gentle, loving teachers.

SHOCK

Unexpected.
Mountain.
Cruel cliffs.

No pitons.
No crampons,
just
bare feet.

Water freezes.
Ice expands.
Pressure builds.
Boulders split.
Glaciers melt.
Shale showers.

Numb.

Angry.
Fearful.
Relieved.
Panicked.
Sleepless.

Irrational.
Anesthetized.
Perceptive.
Courageous,
then a stoic hazy-blur
or
possibly even
the peace-filled clarity
of my time on this peak.

This can't be real.

Disbelief grabs,
time suspends
in this cold dark
summit's spell.

RECOGNITION

Even though
we didn't know,
wouldn't know . . .
for hours.

We stood
in our office.
Bill held me,
we prayed:

"Dear Lord,
give us strength
to help those who need us."

"Let us remember we are growing
through the experience ahead.
Please hold all of us
in Your Light and Love."

We drove home
to be with Dawna.

She needed to know.

We needed
to be together.

Derek
was likely
on one of the planes
that had collided
down the valley.

We waited.

The three of us waited.

Waiting,
I kept
refocusing
my awareness
on God's Light and Love
around them, through
those first hours
of their transition.

ANGELS AND ASHES

Angel clouds
dancing,
coconut sorbet swirls
floated onto that cloudless
dusking sky.

Angels
welcoming
the departed travelers
celebrating
in that lemon,
      apricot,
      raspberry,
      boysenberry sunset.

I saw a vision

of the instant after
the collision.

His death.

Rising
from
twisted
burning
wreckage,
he turned,
extending his hand
to the others,
saying,
"Come on,
don't hold back.
We all have jobs to do."

They
flew on,
leaving
the old clothes,
their bodies
behind in the ashes.

UNTITLED

Unknown to me
seventeen die in midair collision.

that evening i see clouds looking
like an ensemble of dancing angels.

miles southward indian peoples say
is where souls depart this land.

preachers of faith and ministers of science
blow tremendous winds about such puzzles
never arriving at the truth.

the clouds extend their arms and move onward.

KARL KEMPTON

Note: *Months after I wrote ANGELS AND ASHES,
the poet Karl Kempton, whom we had not known,
asked if we would like a copy of a poem
he had written the day Derek died.
This is his untitled poem.*

See acknowledgment on page 268.

OUR CHILD IS DEAD

Those parts of Bill,
those parts of me,
a thousand facets
uniquely shone
in our child.

Loved.
Nurtured.
Vanished.

We thought
we had given
the world this son
to carry on:
lessons,
values,
love,

he vanished,
in *one* moment.

Gone.

Why live on?

GONE

On the slope
of one of the hills
encircling us,
he left this life
of thirteen years
in an instant.

The plane
collided midair
with another
on its climb
into that
aqua silk
sky.

Moments before
at the boarding gate
he gave me one of those
almost grown-up,
almost embarrassed
"I-want-to,
 but-not-here-Mom" hugs.

Waving
good-bye
as he turned,
the light of his smile
filled the space between us.

My last words
still echo off our hills,
"Have a wonderful time, Derek.
We love you."

       You

          you

            you

              bounce

         back to me

   endlessly.

WHY THAT NIGHT?

My lifelong pattern
of sleeping well

broke

a year
before
you died.

Increasing
restlessness.

Strange shifts
started slowly,
imperceptibly.

Checking
children
as I came
down the hall.

Derek
first,
nearest
the door,
then
Dawna.

A gentle touch,
then a whisper,
"We love you."

They must
have heard me,
a smile
would cross each face.

Living room,
stoke the fire,
read or work
awhile.

Productive
project hours
mixed with
looking in on
children
several
times.

I never
asked myself,
"Why do I feel
this growing need
to touch them?"

No fear,
it just felt
warmly *"mothery"*
to see, to know
they were sleeping
peacefully.

Less,

less sleep,
and
less sleep.

Yet
I would
awaken, rested,
as their 4:30 alarm
started a new day with chores.

Strangely

that night,

the night
of the day
you died,
tranquil,
uninterrupted
sleep

returned.

MOURNING AFTER

I awoke,
aware of
mourning
the morning
after you died.

Yet I was
in a river of light,
floating unobstructed
in high, fast energy.

Effortlessly,
synchronized with
the flow of life,
the lives of those around me,
even those unmet, unknown.

As if floodgates had opened . . .

> Memorial service
> arrangements,
> details
> flowed
> together
> as did my words
> as I stood to speak
> to those who
> had come
> to celebrate you.

Then, as days moved to weeks,

> A parking space
> or someone pulling out,
> *always* where I needed to park.

> Impossible
> in our town.
> Yet that's how it was.

> Phone
> would ring
> as I reached to dial.
> It would be the person
> I was calling.

People
I needed to see
I'd meet by *accident?*

Poems
suddenly
began to flow
from my heart
spontaneously
through my pen.

Sheer
openness
kept me from
timidly holding
what I wouldn't have had
the courage to share before.

Leaving
my body,
part of me
would watch
my pain and growth,
until that healing peace returned.

Answers
would come before
questions were asked.

Decisions,
accurate leaps,
all facts considered
seemingly without aim.

Vision.
I saw.
I knew a friend was pregnant
and would
have a daughter,
the child
she had *exactly*
nine months later.

Intuition:
poignant
crystals,
vivid,
trusted
by those around me.

Now,
all important,
each moment,
each person,
precious,
unique.

I was
strangely
unaware of time.

The light
was consistent,
almost frighteningly so
during those first six months.

I moved
with this river
into a new world.

When briefly
clouded in storm,
tears came,
then cleared
to a rainbow.

Connectedness
new to me,
yet
now I know
it has always been.

Bewildered.

Why me?

Why now?

A friend
spoke wisdom,

"This will change.
It did for me.
Unless you choose
to stay in light."

Reminded of my childhood song.

  "This light that I have
      the world didn't give to me.
    What the world didn't give
          the world can't take away."

As months pass,
a simple melody,
that little song
often returns me to
the synchronistic river.

OUR VALLEY

Our hills
hold us.
We cry gently.

They whisper
seasonal melodies.

I am a child
cradled and lulled
in my mother's arms.

Hills and friends
still surround,
softly comfort us.

We deeply
appreciate
all of you,
the prayers,
support, and concern,
from you, our friends,
in this gentle valley.

These
encircling hills
remind me that
we are truly held
in His
everlasting arms.

HOLDING YOU

The morning after
your memorial service.

I stopped
at the mortuary
to get your ashes –
cremains.

I needed
to hold you.
after you died.

Wasn't it only yesterday,
I held you in my arms
after you were born
when your father
drove us home.

I needed
to bring you
home once more.

The box
was heavier
than I expected.

I felt
unforgettably
connected to you
as I held it
on my lap.

The car drove
the familiar road home
as if on automatic pilot.

My only memory
of that trip
is holding
your box.

You were home again.

Home again
here on the farm
in this valley.

Through tears,
cherished memories,
timeless words
blended into comfort.

We each
held the box
of your ashes.

Then
the heavy
little box
was gently
placed to rest
here on the farm

in this land you loved.

LATER

"Remember,
your time
will be
later,
alone."

Everyone needed me.

Decisions,
       decisions,
              decisions.

Often their greatest
need
was to help.
Doing something
dissipates anguish,
despair.

I had to learn
to accept,
not to resist,
a need to help.

New resilience
came, as I learned
of death and grief,
responding to others.

A list
assisted
as I answered,
"What can I do?"

Friends
visited;
dust,
cook,
dishes,
firewood.
They aided
my healing.
Their healing
came, in part,
as they helped.

The hard work of grief
was ahead of me,
alone.

She was right.

"Your time will be later, alone."

It was later,

much, much later.

And alone.

BONDED

My heart

screams

again
when I hear
of your child
missing or dead.

I am
bonded
to you my sisters,
        my brothers.
I feel
I hear
your anguish
across all time,
        all lands.

At least
I know what happened . . .

50,000 missing in Guatemala.
50,000 people disappeared?
. . . no answers anywhere?

Grocery bags.
Milk cartons.
Famine, torture, war,
Nicaragua, Ethiopia, Afghanistan,
row upon row, gravestones
march across my life,
our world.

You, too,
have placed
your child's name
on a missing list
or on a grave.

You, too,
have asked,
"Why go on?"

My soul embraces you.

Notes on my own memories of shock . . .

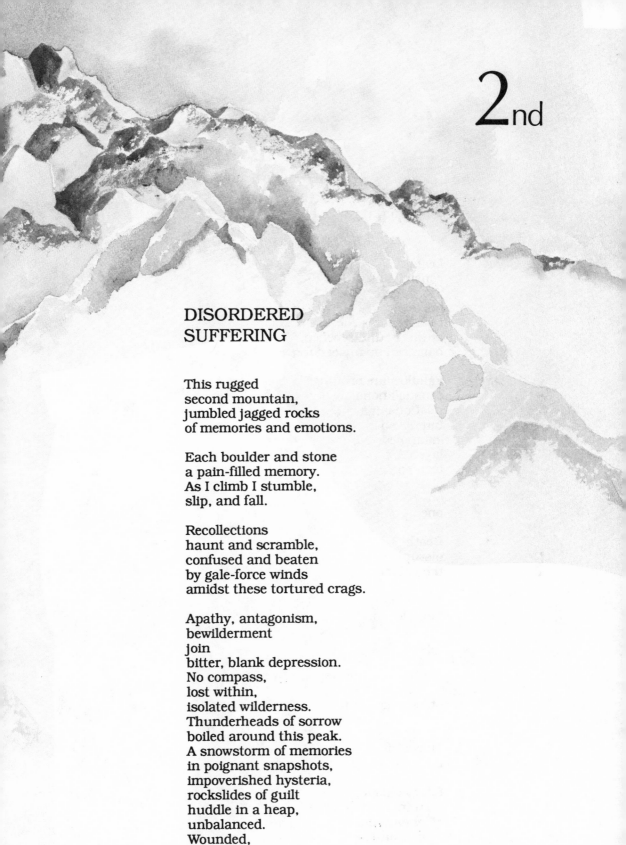

DISORDERED
SUFFERING

This rugged
second mountain,
jumbled jagged rocks
of memories and emotions.

Each boulder and stone
a pain-filled memory.
As I climb I stumble,
slip, and fall.

Recollections
haunt and scramble,
confused and beaten
by gale-force winds
amidst these tortured crags.

Apathy, antagonism,
bewilderment
join
bitter, blank depression.
No compass,
lost within,
isolated wilderness.
Thunderheads of sorrow
boiled around this peak.
A snowstorm of memories
in poignant snapshots,
impoverished hysteria,
rockslides of guilt
huddle in a heap,
unbalanced.
Wounded,
weeping.
Angry.

RELATIONSHIP

Living
constellates
my life into
one-on-one
relationships,
attracted and repelled,
balanced by unseen forces.

Families are orbiting
constellations of
relationships
interlaced,
entangled,
layered,
teamed
one-
on-
one.

Death
disrupts
the balance.

Those left
must let go.

I must let go,

        shift perspective,

one has gone on.

Those left
grieve alone.

I grieve alone,
even in a loving family
of one-on-one
   one-on-one
   one-on-one
   relationships.

KICKED

Death kicked
our family box.

Four sides
now three.

A triangle
is not a
box.

IS IT?

Death isn't fair.

It isn't fair.

It isn't fair.

Is it?

IN TRIPLICATE
IN TRIPLICATE
IN TRIPLICATE

Our mail comes
to an old brown barn mailbox
with a rusty red metal flag.

I stop
to get the mail,
turning onto
our well-worn dirt road
into this valley.

In the mail . . .
A thick envelope.
Return address –
Health Department.

Of course . . .
The long-awaited Water Report.
Why does it take so long to get reports?
I open it.
My eyes fly
to typed words,
look for "acceptable"
quantity and quality.

First word
stops my eyes,

sears into my memory.

My breath
vanishes,
vacuumed out,
instant nausea,
vomiting,
days of depression,
reeling out of balance.

The death certificate,
    in triplicate
        in triplicate
            in triplicate . . .

ANGRY

It should have been me.

A child doesn't die

before

his

mother.

Abandoned.

Not once but twice.

I live on.

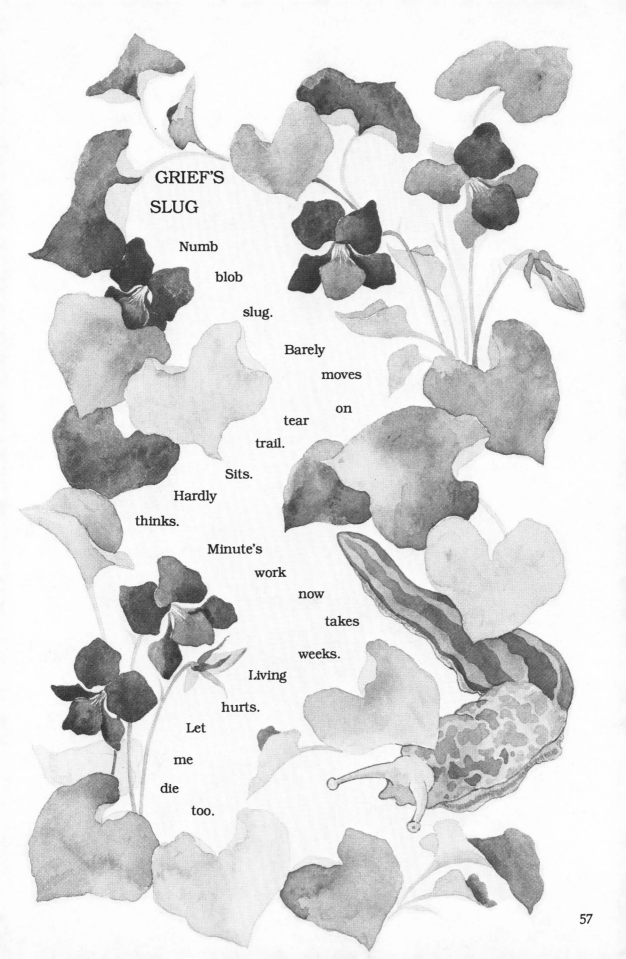

GRIEF'S SLUG

Numb

blob

slug.

Barely

moves

on

tear

trail.

Sits.

Hardly

thinks.

Minute's

work

now

takes

weeks.

Living

hurts.

Let

me

die

too.

GRANDPARENTS

Your Grandchild dead.

Your child an amputee,
not of limb but heart
maimed of purpose
life meaning
gone.

Your dreams,
your hopes,
your name
will not
live on.

Grandmother,
grandfather
has anyone
recognized
your pain?

IN COSTUME

My old friend
Guilt
kept
coming by,
knocking on my door,
wearing masks.

Look closer.

Guilt
is
fear,
masquerading.

Look even closer.

Face
illusion,
insecurity,
fear of lack,
      pain,
      attack,
      abandonment.

In asking "Why?"
the impostor
is found,
examined,
cannot
stay.

When
I see guilt
for what it is,
"Here's that fear, again,"

then
peace-filled love
calmly opens the door.

Without
a word,
Guilt

turns,

skulks

away.

ONE IN TEN

"Only one in ten marriages
survives the wrenching trauma
of the death of a child."

Those words
plunge into me
through the fog of pain.

Trauma,
a magnifying glass,
enlarging tiny flaws.
Uncapped toothpaste tube
suddenly becomes
a gaping infected wound.
Anthill is now
a craggy mountain.
It looms above me
in an 8.5 earthquake.

Nothing
stays in balance,
the whole world reels.
Reference points vanish,
    s
            h
                a
                    t
                        t
Staying   e
concurrent
is impossible.   r.
Each person in the family
is spinning on a different axis,
        at different speeds,
        in different orbits
        of understanding.

Death makes an earthquake,
powerful pain-filled tremors
within each person's core,
sudden magma shifts
too deep to be detected.
Volcanoes erupt,
devastating
everyone
in sight.

We tried to go it alone.

Please hear me,
"Get help – good help.
It's there,
reach out
early."

Grief
seems
to separate

men

and

women.

Grieving
patterns
tend to differ.

People keep saying,
"But you have each other."
Oh, how little,
Oh, how little they know.

The things
one understands,
needs to talk about
are uncomfortable,
bring tears
or anger
for the other.

Listening to,
supporting Dawna
is the only aspect of our grief
we have done easily
together.

Hold on,

talk to each other,
give yourselves time,
there *will be* aftershocks.

Marriages that make it are often stronger.

OUT OF MY BODY

When I start
a slide down
my mountain
into tears,
part of me
slips out
above me,
beyond
reach.

Hovers.

Watches.

Waits.

RETURNING

My soul,
my spirit
encounters
all lives, all time.

Recharged,
it returns
refreshed
from floating free
with wholeness and joy
beyond this life,
beyond any one
life.

I know
I am not my body.
I am free, as God created me.

ETCHED WORDS

A thousand times
I saw it at your waist.
Those words went unnoticed.

Now,
as I hold
your buckle
even twisted and burned –
it tells me a triumphant story.

"Race Completed,"
etched in metal,
quietly speaks to me
of each day lived fully.

Life
for you
was a "Ride and Tie."

You left no day,
no business,
no relationship unfinished.

Your race was completed.

HATCHING

Yesterday
I held an egg.

A tiny chick
began pecking

slowly,

slowly,

slowly,

pecking its way out
of the shell
to set
itself
free.

Today,
I see
each of us,
like the chick
inside the egg,
ready to emerge
free.

Why am I
so happy and excited
when a chick sets itself free,
yet feel so abandoned
knowing that Derek
left his shell?

He left me
here
in my shell.

He is free.

I, too,
will hatch
before long.

THE SEED

How does it know?

This little seed,
how does it know

to become a weed,
a tree,
or
a rose?

How does it know?

DAWNA DAVIES
written at age 6

See acknowledgment on page 268.

LAUGHTER

When my mind starts to wander,
the first thing I hear
is laughter.

Endless ripples,
like the water
in the creek.

I can hear their laughter –
brother and sister
partners
friends
as they throw meadow muffin frisbees at each other
       dive into the cattle drinking hole
       run and splash in the sprinklers
       play ball in the field
       squirt each other in a milking "Star Wars"
       ride up the hill on the horses
       razz each other doing chores
       share a picnic lunch
       build their "secret fort"
       hunt frogs, turtles, crawdads
       fish in the creek
       bike to the beach
       poke and fuss in the car
       run when late for the school bus,
              as their cows come
              to the fence
              to say hello,
    talk in their room.

What's funny about a fart?

Yes, I hear their laughter . . .

THE DINNER PARTY

Two children,
eight and ten,
ask, "Can we cook
    if we invite
    company
    for dinner?"

Both have specialties,
favorite dishes
they prepare.
One dish,
maybe two,
but a whole meal?

That's this story.

Menu decisions:
      Color – red
           green
           yellow.

    Balance – bread and cereal
           milk and meat
           fruits and vegetables
           sweet for treat.

Four supply lists:
      garden
      freezer
      on hand
      market.

Who does what? When?
Both clean up their own mess.

Menu:

Goat cheese they made themselves.

Dawna – Flaming spinach apple salad.

Derek – Pasta homemade! Fresh and tender.

Dawna – Roast pork from a pig they raised.

Dawna – Wheat bread, fresh from the oven.

Derek – Butter from our Jersey cow's cream,
        bright yellow naturally;
        no color need be added.

Dawna – Green beans, garden fresh with her
        hollandaise sauce.

Derek – Corn, run from the field to the kitchen.

Derek – Lemon pie, a mountain of meringue,
        ten home-grown egg whites tall.
        It looked like San Luis Peak,
        road and all.

The children had been
Mr. and Mrs. Madonna's
requested dinner guests
at their eclectic
Madonna Inn.

Turnabout.

There's no doubt,

Alex and Phyllis
will always remember
milking and chores,
then dinner on our farm.

TEARS IN FOOD

Food –
the kitchen,
the store,
the dining table –

is where grief still confronts me.

I couldn't face the kitchen,
  once the heart of our home.
I felt trapped
  in a cage of grief
  when I tried to cook.
I cried and cried.
I avoided the store until
  there was absolutely nothing
  but mustard in the refrigerator,
  then
I cried
  up and down
  each market aisle.
I cried inside
  while I tried to eat,
  looking at the exquisite porcelain heart
  on our kitchen table,
  made in memory of him.
  It holds forget-me-nots.
For thirteen years
Derek and food
went together,
nourishing us.

I miss his mischievousness.

I even miss the crawdads
  and fish from the creek
  startling me in the sink.

I miss his help.

I miss his going with me for groceries.
I miss his picking the salad from our garden.
I miss his pasta, both Cuisinarts whirling at once.
I miss his canning with all the family.
I miss his setting the table.
I miss his eating with us.

I miss *him*.

I don't cry so much now.
I'm learning to serve food without tears.

THANK YOU

How did you
always remember
to say "Thank you"?

No matter how
small or large
the help we gave,
you made sure
we felt, we knew
it was appreciated.

Even
as a toddler,
it was
as if you knew
you might not have
the chance to say "tank oo"
again, another day.

Then
you grew tall –
so near a man –
yet all boy
and
still
so kind,
so thoughtful.

Of all those "Thank you's,"
the one
I miss,
remember most,
is "Thanks,
   Mom,
   for dinner.
   It tasted good". . .

as
     you
          touched
               my
                    shoulder
                         softly.

THE RING

Just
weeks
before
his death,
he found a ring.

A ring
like ripples
in a stream of gold.

"Mom,
would you
wear this ring?"

He slipped
it on my finger
with "It looks like a mountain,
     with a hill and a valley.
     Just like life,
     isn't it,
     Mom?"

The tiny ring fit perfectly.

Had an unknown jeweler
made it
for
my
finger?

Where did it come from?

It was just there on the ground.

Derek,
I thought
you'd like to know.

The ring
is still where
you
slipped it
on my finger.

YOUR ROPE

The only rope you left
is an old one
you didn't like.

You packed the rest.

Your bag disintegrated
with your body
in the crash.

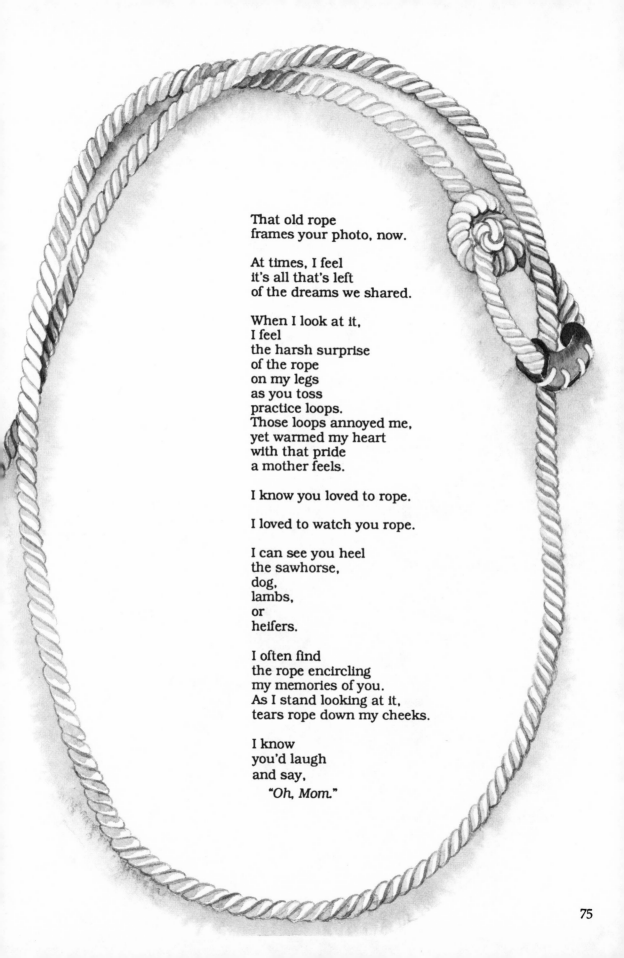

That old rope
frames your photo, now.

At times, I feel
it's all that's left
of the dreams we shared.

When I look at it,
I feel
the harsh surprise
of the rope
on my legs
as you toss
practice loops.
Those loops annoyed me,
yet warmed my heart
with that pride
a mother feels.

I know you loved to rope.

I loved to watch you rope.

I can see you heel
the sawhorse,
dog,
lambs,
or
heifers.

I often find
the rope encircling
my memories of you.
As I stand looking at it,
tears rope down my cheeks.

I know
you'd laugh
and say,
   "Oh, Mom."

SKIP AND BOOTS

Your old dog Skip is greyer now,
yet sturdy and staunch he stands.
Chore boots, cracked and weathered,
bid "Welcome home" from our porch.
Skip still barks as a plane flies over
as he did when you were here.

He was a cuddly fluff of a pup
when outgrown boots in the rack
were joined by those larger and new.
As the chore cycle closed,
racked and upended washed boots
stood drying and ready to wear.

Dawn's frost crystals crunch under boots
as when you and Skip walked to the barn.
His ears always lift at the drone
of a distant plane or of one drawing near.
The bark brings that thought.
Could he know a plane took you away?

Now your old dog Skip
lies among flowers graveside.
His crusted nose on his paw,
his eyes watch the porch
where your old chore boots
stand as dusty gray guards.

"MESSIAH," MILK, MONEY, MOZART

Music shared is magnified.

Music
on a family farm
may not mesh with milk
until you hear two children
singing Handel's "Messiah"
a cappella,
as they merrily milk
their cows and goats.
A munching medley
with the metronome
of a milking machine
on a still moonlit morn.

The moos of cows
    mantras of pigs,
        goats,
        sheep,
        chickens,
   frogs from the creek
merge with mist
or moaning wind,
    coyotes wail matins.

At times
you can hear
the moan of an oboe
meticulously playing
a modicum of Mozart.

Madrigals to barbershop,
"The Messiah" to country western,
show tunes to camp songs,
hymns of praise.
We sang them all.

Mozart Festival
each year, principal oboist
sponsored by two children
with their milking money.

"Messiah"
Milk
Money
Mozart
Music
    Music
       Music.

GIRLS

Football,
roping cows,
horses,
even
your dog,
still came
before girls.

Yet
your head
turned
as they
walked by.

You enjoyed
their phoning you,
as girls now do.

We knew
some girls
had been
very
special,
too.

I smile
today,
motherly
judgment
suspended,
where once
I would have
frowned.
We found
two copies of
Playboy
among
your treasures.

You

were

a thirteen-

year-old boy.

HOW MANY PRETZELS?

Remember dancing?

Four of us,
Dawna and you,
Dad and I.

We danced
all kinds;
we liked
western dancing
best.
Not square dancing,
but western swing.

You and Dawna race
to finish milking
and other chores,
then race again,
getting ready
to go dancing.

I can still
smell
your Dad's
aftershave lotion
on you.

I can still
see
that freshly washed,
meticulously combed hair,
such
a change from
the haystack
of blond straight hair
we usually saw you wear.

I can still
see
the two of you
dancing out
across the floor.

I loved to dance
with you,
but
even more,
I loved to watch you
dance with Dawna.

You learned to follow,
feel the rhythm.
Then to lead.

As you found the need,
you two learned,
then together taught,
  Swing
  10-Step
  27-Step
  Cowboy Two
  Schottische
  Texas Two-Step
  Cotton-Eyed-Joe
  Polka
  Windmill
  Windshield Wiper
  Yo-Yo
  Waltz
  Cuddle
  Freeze
  Cowboy Two
  Triple-Step
  Duck Under
  Deanna Lynn
  Cowboy Two, again
  Aggie Stomp
  Triple-Step
  Shuffle Dance
  Two-Step Swing
  and
  The Pretzel.

Remember the night you taught 80 couples to Pretzel?

DANCING IN BOOTS

Over
the years
we danced
in the moonlight,
under the stars,
on polished dance floors,
in parking lots or patios,
even in the kitchen to the radio.

Smooth worn
leather soles
on cowboy boots
slid across those floors.
Even with heels on boots
your sun-streaked hair
barely topped my belt buckle
when we started to dance together.

Tall and short,
Dad and Dawna, you and I,
often caused a chuckle or two.

Your boots
always looked too big,
until
suddenly
after all those years

you were

as tall
as I.

Size 10 1/2
grounded you well
even at 5 feet 8.

It no longer
looked and felt
awkward to be held,
                      twirled,
dipped, swung, spun, or
whirled away in your arms.

With hair
blown dry,
clean jeans,
polished boots,
you looked,
even smelled,
so near a man,
but still a boy,
my son.

Our son . . .

Though
Dad and I
loved to watch
you dance with Dawna,
I felt proud and pleased

when you'd coltishly
toss your head
and invite

"Mom, let's dance."

I'm sure you're still dancing.

Do you know
how I long to hear
those words
again?

"Mom, let's dance."

IT'S YOUR BIRTHDAY

February 5, 1985

Dear Derek,

You
were born easily
fourteen years ago this evening.

I still smile
at the doctor's words:
"I love you farm girls.
You come without fears,
lie down and have a baby
like the cows who taught you how."

You
came easily,
lived easily,
learned easily,
loved easily,
left easily.

You
touched in
often enough;
there could be
no doubt you were real.
You'd pester, taunt, tease Dawna
as a brat, a boy, a little brother.

You
already
understood so much.
I often wondered,
were you raising me?

You
met us,
taught us
on our ground,
not asking us
to come to yours.

You
always
seemed to know
where you were needed.

You
were
meeting
my needs,
while I thought
I was meeting yours.

You
were clear
on what was important,
easily adjusted your focus
as new light came into the picture,
like dawn into a new day.

You
knew
what was
right and wrong.
It seemed you brought it
with you
from somewhere else,
used it here
most of the time.

Your
clarity
made you
determined,
difficult at times.
When I didn't understand,
you knew what was important.

Life forced few tears from you.

You
moved cautiously,
rarely falling,
even as you began to walk.

You'd just sit down gently.

You
understood
choice,
its role in life.

No need complaining.

Watching
where one is going
is a choice.

Would
you
still
be with us
had the pilots
heard you
as you often said,
"When I watch
where I'm going
won't fall,
get hurt"?

You
mastered
the lessons
this life held.

Somehow
knowing this
makes it possible
to accept your flight . . .

Yes,
clarity,
caution,
thoughtfulness
were gifts you gave us
as your stream of life
blended with ours
for a while
and now flows on.

Lovingly and thankfully,

Mom

Note: *This letter was actually where I discovered
writing would be a helpful healing tool for me.
This was the first piece I wrote.*

Notes of remembering . . .

NEW ORDER

Suddenly
peak three
stood ahead of me.

Recognition
of the finality
in a fatality
joins new expression,
inconsistently
moving toward
reconnecting,
re-entry.

Watch out.

An avalanche
suddenly breaks loose.
Joltingly vivid recollections
knocked me down,
did not crush me.

Where will I get
the energy to go on?

Painful flashbacks
punctuate evolving order.
Reorganization appears
as we work our way
up and over
summit
three.

Four steps forward,
one or maybe five back,
yet somehow
reinvolvement comes.

GRIEF'S LIGHTS

Light,
the sun,
the moon,
the stars,
change how I see.

Light can blind me,
is all I see.

Grief blinds me.

At first
that's all I see,
then grief
changed how
and what I saw.

Its floodlight
shone directly
in my face.

Now
it follows me
   staulks me
   haunts me
   taunts me.

I can no more
run from grief
than from sunlight
            moonlight
            starlight.

Even
man-made lights
follow me.

Car lights.
Firelights.
Candlelights.
Beacon lights.

Neon lights
on and off
flash
waves
of grief.

Airplane lights,
even
airplane sounds
once unnoticed,
now surround.
No escape,
everywhere I go,
they hum like bees.
Birds by day,
by night
they look like stars.

The rheostat
of time
slowly
dims
grief's rays.

Now those
lights expand
my range of vision.

They've profoundly changed
how and what I see.

Who escapes?

CHANGING HILLS

Halt my hurry,
tune into life.
At points of change,
even points of pain,
find new depth in living.

These hills reflect
changes in my life.

California hills
change gently.

Against these hills
time and life
are fragile
now.

Winter's
tune of rain
played on our roof
as the road washed out,
and our bridge disappeared underwater.

Then new grass jumped
overnight from dampened soil.
A lush fairyland of green velvet carpet
draped the shoulders of our Irish Hills.

So vivid,
my breath taken –
Can this be real?

I pinch myself.
Is this Heaven?

Spring
wind-spun
windmill.
Water-filled
gray tanks
on the hill
sloshed over
as a ten-foot waterfall.
Tender green
crescendoed
into a symphony,
vibrantly performed
in blue
      lavender
        magenta
          rose
            yellow
            and poppy-gold
wildflowers on the slopes.

Summer
turns the hills amber.
The wind pulses a soft rock song
on grass and croplands.
Fields of grain wave,
a gentle reminder
of Derek's
wind-tousled
blond hair.

Tears fall
as I recall
years I watched
from our kitchen window
as I made cheese, butter or dinner
while he ran across those pastures
with his sister, as day turned dusk,
their dog, calves, goats and kids
frolicking behind.

Autumn's
endless rhythms,
harvest sounds:
grinding grain
snapping beans
shucking corn
chopping stalks
whirring fruit dryer
simmering apple butter
boiling canning kettle
popping lids.

To remind me
there should be
time for resting,
the hills take on a patina of age,
that gray-brown hue
of time and weather
on an unpainted barn.

Unharvested
seeds fall,
waiting for rain.

Between
autumn and winter
I am in another
season of awareness.

Holiday's
earthbound stars
color the hillsides,
bring joy and heartache
to each day of this season.
Lights, like twinkling jewels,
shine through my loving tears.

Memories
jolt me painfully,
then cradle me as I cry.
With passing time
tears are both
the dew of pain
and
pearls
of remembrance.

Our hills
share their
changing melodies.
The seasons remind me
change has purpose,
is valuable,
recognized,
shared.

A PROBLEM

The toughest time?

Christmas night.

I saw it coming.

If Christmas Day
is a tricky wrinkle,
by Christmas evening
it is bound to be
a sticky wicket.

"Please come over."

You are welcome
at our Open House;
dessert, singing, sharing.
Bring your honest
gift of sadness
and at least one
beautiful Christmas memory
to bare and share together.

You'll have a Christmas
worth remembering
when you discover
Christmas
in your heart.

Christmas,
once known,
must be rediscovered.
A birth,
life begins again today,
each day,
each Christmas.

Now Christmas evening,
sharing,
caring with others
is a pleasant
        laughing
            cheerful heart of Christmas.

Not a problem,

Christmas.

BACK-TO-SCHOOL NIGHT 1985

A few moments
on the high school campus,
I'm screaming inside in anguish.

What's happening to me?

Everyone
is laughing,
   talking,
   saying "Hello."

No one else
sees or feels
the torturous explosions,

flashing neon lights of anger
in pitch-dark night.

Dreams
shattered,
burned with your body,
when two airplanes
collided, crashed
over a year ago.

But dreams of this year
slipped by me unnoticed,
then jumped out of the dark 1

   screaming
tonight.

Why aren't you here?

Derek, this was the year.
Dawna's senior year.
Your freshman year.

You and she were more than anxious
to be in school together,
again.

Only twenty months in age
and Dawna's skip in grade
had kept you
in separate schools
six whole years.

Finally,
together
in school
one last year.

Years of walking
running
or biking
to the school bus
were going to end.

Dawna is driving now.

You two,
driving.
On your own.
Independent,
laughing,
talking,
best friends,
sharing secrets,
fun being together,
business partners,
dancing partners,
brother and sister.

I didn't realize
the together dreams
were living on . . . band,
                  choir,
                  tours,
              stage choir,
           double-dating,
          youth symphony,
       international jazz festival,
    football, basketball, baseball games,
livestock shows, fairs and rodeos . . .

It's Back-to-School Night 1985.

You are supposed to be here, *Derek.*

WAITING

Why can't I stop

looking
at the sky . . .

watching
for the door . . .

listening
for your footsteps . . .

waiting
for your voice
           smile
              or touch?

How
many times
does my heart
have to flare with joy?

I see you,

then

         it

s   falls,
  h
      a
          t
            t
              e
                r
                  e
                      d
on the floor

when I find
he's not you.

I see you
across the room,
down in the field,
roping in the arena,
running along the beach,
in a movie in the theater,
biking along country roads,
blond hair tousled by the wind,
even wearing the jacket
you wore *that* day . . .

Sometimes
you are a little boy,
oftentimes a teen,
at times a man.
Yet always
my son.

It's

you

coming
down the street,
the Mother's Day
bouquet in hand,

the dozen
yellow roses
you so proudly
brought to me
this day last year.

I still can't believe
you are not coming home.

Today is Mother's Day.

TIME

Must I do
things that
don't get done?

Derek's
death

stopped me,

made me
look
at
life.

When
what
I feel
I need to do
doesn't fit in,

I need to ask myself

why
I
need
to do it.

Often
I find
if I let
someone
else do it,

I meet their needs.

NOT GETTING LOST

I had
to learn
to live
without seeing you.

Coping with
just one moment,
one hour,
one day,
helped me not get lost
as I learned to live again.

Are my
choices today
in line with
a lifetime of love and peace?

"Living Intentionally,"
the course we organized,
taught as a family team,
still works for me
though you're growing
on another plane of being.

Seven
balance points,
we said.
Each is important,
even in life's worst traumas.

Seven areas.
Choices *written*
helped me keep balance,
find peace,

as I spun, swirled, reeled,
engulfed in traumatic growth.

SPIRITUAL
  Leaps in understanding
        come with study, prayer and thought.
        Refreshing. Renewing.
        The lesson, Sunday,
        the "Daily Word,"
        the "Course,"
        my quiet time.
  I begin again each week, each day.

FAMILY
  It's hard
        learning to be
        three, no longer four.
        We're making it slowly,
        with difficulties at times.

  We backpacked through snow
        on the Pacific Crest Trail
        into Uncle Patt's camp last weekend.
  You would have loved that trip.

PHYSICAL
  Exercise,
        good diet,
        enough rest,
        recognizing anger,
        acknowledging stress,
        venting grief with writing;
        each helped me stay in good health.

PERSONAL
  Pleasures
        just for me;
        taking classes,
        breaking a colt,
        working at the ranch,
        redoing my wardrobe,
        changing my hair style,
        reading a book a month,
        learning to let go of
        my fear of writing.

PROFESSION

Keeping in touch
    with pulse points
    of my work
    required constant effort.
No new projects, thank you.

HOME

Think in terms of one day,
    one hour.
Sometimes
all I can handle
are five-minute blocks of time.
    Five minutes:
      Dust,
      Water plants,
      Make a salad,
      Set the table,
      Wash one window,
      Clean the bathroom,
      Straighten the living room,
      Unload-reload the dishwasher.

A calm, inspiring home still takes effort.
The new house you wanted
    to help build is coming along.
Our farm is simplified,
    can almost be handled without you.

SOCIAL

Helping others with grief
    has helped me grow.
We're still dancing,
    though short a partner.
I speak often about WORLD NEIGHBORS
    and Third World Development.
A master's degree is still a long-term goal.

Choices
written out in all seven areas
each month,
checked each week.
Steadied me.

A sense of balance
allowed me not to get lost
this most difficult
year of my life,
my first year
without you.

A FILLY
AND
WRANGLERS

Your new Wranglers
were being washed
the day you flew.

Those 27 x 34's,
now a faded blue.
The filly and I
have nearly worn
them out for you.

One day a week.
Thursday, the day
I save to be with her,
                with you.

We do the things
you and I love so much:
gather cattle off the hills,
bring in A I. cows,
sort and doctor,
work the chute.

I started her at two.
Now she's coming three.
Light, quick and easy
as we work those cows.
She trots to the gate
when she hears me
call across the field.

She's a dream come true.
Your Dad gave her to me
for our nineteenth
wedding anniversary.

Even faded blue
Wranglers and a filly
bring an important
spot of balance
in my life.
As I adjust
to not seeing you.

CELEBRATING SEASONS

For years
on season's change
we have stopped and
shared with others.

We have potluck parties.
Friends from across the fence
and around the world
gather in our living room.

From their scrapbook of memories
each shares verbally or through music
a glimpse of the coming season.

Without celebrating,
here on the California coast,
spring blends into
summer,
autumn,
winter,
all unnoticed.

Another year

whooshed by me.

Take note.
Find
most life responds
to the sun,
to the earth's tilt.

Celebrate the change with us.
What does the new season mean?

Bring two things:
a dish towards dinner
and a poem,
        object,
        song,
        or your thoughts
        of the coming season . . .

Summer
may mean
sandals,
endless energy,
long lazy days,
sweat on brow,
a zucchini explosion
if the seeds
you planted
numbered more than one.

Autumn
nippy air,
school begins,
golden pumpkins,
butterflies come home
to the eucalyptus grove.

Winter
snowfall,
chilly chores,
holiday hustle,
quiet contemplation.

Spring
daffodils,
those telephones to God.

Each
sees,
hears,
feels,
remembers
differently.
Words, music,
sharing widen
our world.

Friends come
whose homeland
has two seasons
instead of four:
wet and dry,
food and famine.

The angle
of the sun
on our world
brings more change
than we often recognize.

Even though you're gone,
seasons are celebrated.

INVESTING IN MEMORIES

Every moment holds a memory.

Remember . . .
each evening
during dinner
we passed verbal photos
of each other's day.

What do you want
to remember about today?
What lessons did life teach you?

Keeping tuned to each other.
Living with antennae
turned to *now*,
shared.

Recalling laughter and tears.
Vignettes, vivid snapshots
of the adventures of your days,
our "scrapbook" is full of memories of you.

Remember . . .
the sweat on your brow
as you pushed the bus out of mud
on that wind-swept Andean mountain road.
At 14,000 feet above the level of the sea,
in oxygen-thin air you helped
a Quechua village farmer.
A glimpse into his life –
the immensity
of his problems.

Their apprehension,
then smiles and laughter
as you taught other children
to milk your goats and cows.

Playing football
with your heart and soul;
the amazement on your face
when they named you
"Player of the Year."

Walt Woodard's shock
was matched only by your own
as you caught on the third go-round
to win your first three-steer roping.

Those wonder-filled three months
we took you both out of school
to trace and touch
our roots across this land.
We each became
part of our nation's history.
We found her grandeur,
her pulsing pride,
her fragility.
Plaguing problems came into focus.

Flying into an Eskimo village
over backs of moose
browsing on snowy tundra
slid time back half a century.
Grandpa and Grandma taught here
on this wilderness edge of the world.

Pulling those defying weeds,
planting innumerable seeds
persistently with Grandma
in the warm California sun.
Selling produce we didn't need
from the back of our old
'55 Ford pickup truck.

The tension and concern
etched your face as you helped
one of your and Dawna's cows
give birth on a cold, stormy night.

The thrill of climbing through
the mist along the Inca Trail
to find ancient mystery
in Machu Picchu.

Memories to remember . . .

Bedtime, talks with God,
those special, private talks.
What shall we thank Him for tonight?

Remembering . . .

You invested in life each day.
You lived more fully in thirteen years
than many people do in a *lifetime*,

partially, because we as a family
invested in memories.

Derek, we still do.

YOU MADE A DIFFERENCE

You saw,
    understood,
    believed,
    made a difference, Derek.

Throughout your thirteen years
you watched WORLD NEIGHBORS *
help our friends,
most of whom we've never met,
have more food,
clean water,
better health,
grow three bags of beans
where only one grew before,
in some cases ten bags instead of one,
because their village asked
WORLD NEIGHBORS' help.

In millions of villages
in still-developing nations
across our earth,
mothers,
fathers,
children
need to learn
to care for their land,
to nurse it carefully,
enabling it to produce
ample food to feed
their families.

They know their land,
climate,
traditions.
They want to solve their problems.

We work together
to find new ways,
new seeds,
and most of all,
a new vision of ourselves
as they teach their neighbors
the methods we learn together
for positive, long-term change.

You understood
the careful tending it takes
to get poor land to produce crops.

In the years
you lived with us
you touched more lives
than we realized.

In fact
people are
still donating
to
WORLD NEIGHBORS
in memory of you,
Derek,
to help continue
the quiet assistance,
creating positive,
appreciated change
in remote villages
across our world.

In death
your love,
your concern for others
continues . . .

Derek,
you are still
making a difference.

*__Note:__ WORLD NEIGHBORS is a nonsectarian
international, private, volunteer organization
which accepts no government funding.

For more information:

WORLD NEIGHBORS
5116 North Portland Ave.
Oklahoma City, OK 73112

ALONE

Today
being alone
is almost sacred.

As morning breaks to dawn,
snuggle into the comfortable chair.
The warmth and crackle of the fireplace
stir new understanding . . .

With the coming light of day
the big black glob
in the living room window
slowly transforms into
a majestic mountain.

Oaks,
rocks,
the deer grazing
come into focus
as concepts and thoughts
take on clarity and form.

Somehow
this is best done alone.

Tears come most easily alone.

Peace and joy
are decisions
I make

alone.

CHOICE

Standing surrounded
by loving people,
I am lonely.

Surprised, I find
I make this choice.

I choose

> to feel sorry for myself
> as a victim of life and death

> or

> to help others understand
> and grow through their griefs,

> to see you critically stare
> at the scar on my face

> or

> to feel your wonder
> at who is behind
> my deep blue eyes,

> to complain of Dawna's
> messy room and unmade bed

> or

> to appreciate the blessing
> she is in my life,

> to think sad thoughts
> of missing Derek

> or

> to think happy thoughts
> remembering the years
> we shared,

> to call for love

> or

> to be loving.

I find
warmth,
security
in seeing
aloneness
as just one
of my choices.

STICKY MUD

To keep
even
one foot
in the stream
required all,
every tiny ounce,
of everything
I could muster.

One foot
stuck in
the sticky
mud of grief.

It is work
to free myself
by not resisting.

Shifting energy.
Shifting my weight.
Shifting my thoughts.
Shifting my perspective.

Now,
wading on more solid footing,
the sticky mud washes off
as I participate
again in
life.

TREES AND PEOPLE

I heard the whisper
of wind in the trees
in this sun-filled meadow.

It said,
"Trees are people."

Trees
stand tall,
usually in couples
or in families,
branches touching.
Yet others stand
by themselves, alone.

Trees
lean on those
around them when ill
or uprooted by a storm.

Trees
die.

Trees
must get
a message
their time here
has come to a close.
Notice,
even they
have a sense of urgency
to leave a mark on time.

A dying pine has a thousand cones.

Trees
experience
transition, death.
Trees have another lifetime.
They burn as light and warmth.
Cut down, they stand again
in barns and buildings.
After all,
they turn once more
into the ever-nurtured land.

"Trees, like people,
have several lifetimes."

I heard this from the wind.

WHY DID I WAIT SO LONG?

Why did I think I couldn't write?

Writing,
always difficult,
always filled with failure,
until . . .

Through foggy numbness,
it came cascading,
as water slips over
the waterfall
into an inlet
in Mirror Lake.
Refreshed
by misting spray,
those relieving tears,
discovered rainbows.

Writing
now lets me play
with words and sounds.

It's a positive way
to pull myself into
a reflective,
sheltered
bay.

Idea,
question,
pondered,
held,
a nascent spring
once locked in rock.

I have something to say.

Writing
 settles thoughts;
s
 e
  d i m
       e   n
             t
              f
               a
                l
                 l
                  s,

                      d
                       r i f
                            t
                             s

Writing   a
and water   w   a
clarify,   y.
expose depth,
reveal unknown dimensions,
as crystal returns light
while passing it on.

Unneeded,
a word let go
is not loss.

Strong.
Crisp.

Even here,
as everywhere,
a teaspoon given
returns
as a cup,
a bucket.

Overflowing . . .

Why did I wait so long?

Releasing, I receive.

Message "swiftens"
by honing the flow.
Its meaning has
more edge.

Writing and water
carve into the cliffs of time.

THE UNDERSTANDING GARDEN

As we walk through life
at points of lessons,
there are joy, pain.

We stop,
      watch,
            feel.
When
we look,
we always find
a flower growing.

Flowers share their understanding:
seeds, bulbs and cuttings.

Understanding,
came home
with us.

In our valley,
there's a knoll
on the sunny bank of the creek
where Grandma planted trees of wisdom.

Flowers grow
among those trees.
Seeds tended lovingly.

Come . . .

sit,
share,
or read.
I am often here.

Come . . .

pick a bouquet
in passing, as you leave.

Notes on emerging order . . .

4th

PERSPECTIVE

It happened.
No struggle.

Life
found me
as I descended
from the rugged peaks
onto this breeze-rumpled hill
of pastures strewn
with wild bloom.

Flowers
I'd not seen before
held answers to
my question,

"Why?"

A new vision
of myself emerged
as I left the mountains.

I examined blooms
on those hilltop fields;
I found answers,
priorities untangled.
Verve transformed into lassitude,
shifted into purpose.

ABOVE THE FOG

Inner sight,
intersight,
insight
not known before.

Somehow
I turned
from confusion,
clutter,
petty memories
of the past
to what is important,
to what I need to do today.
A vision of my role
in moving toward
a less fearful,
less painful
world.

He was a gentle teacher.

He learned easily,
not needing to climb through
the garbage of mistakes
and unlearning
as most
of us do.

Did he bring the wisdom
of many lifetimes
when he came
to live
with us?

Clarity,
a gift he gave,
a gift of good-bye.

I need to use it.

When I do,
it's as though
I am standing
on a mountain
above the fog,

seeing

forever.

HIS MOTHER AND ME

When
I stay
tuned to
my whole self,
I feel
no sense
of separation
from Derek.

Only
when I
separate myself
into

his mother

and

me,

do I find

pain and sadness.

WE EACH SWING

Had I fallen into an ice-fed lake?

A jolt,
a shock
showered over me
as I began to see
loving
     or
calling for help
as two points
between which we swing.

A peace-filled
     or
pain-filled
choice.

People love
by listening
with compassion
and gentle joy.
We care,
nurture,
accept
     or
swing to
a call for help,
actually
a call for love.
Illness – guilt
roots in fear.

See,
hear
and feel
that fear.
Guilt attacks,
as does pain, anger,
hate, jelousy, even crime.
All these are calls for love.

Loving behavior
is comfortable.

Comfort tells.

Isn't that the meaning
in these timeless words:
"Love is patient and kind . . ."
"Love does not demand its own way."
"Love goes on forever."

When I see,
hear or feel
a call for love
coming from me
or anyone,
I can choose
to swing
to a loving perspective
    or
I can choose
to stay
in my own call for love.

A little call
still calls.

Now life,
even nations,
and our world
look different
when those ugly labels
good and bad
are replaced by
caring and fearing
    or
loving and calling for love.

No mystery.
Simply a miracle.
Our perception shifts
as we swing
from a call for love
to loving.

Isn't this what Christ was saying?

The ill become well.
Fear dissolves in love.
Life moves on
to new levels.

LISTENING

"Why
haven't
I written
more of anger,
when anger is such
a consuming
part of grief?"

I have a connected picture
of life and death,
of faith and peace.

My lifelong commitment
to live life now
keeps me recognizing,
acknowledging my thoughts.

When anger
appears,

I sit down,
listen.

Anger
resisted
is enticed,
strengthened.
As are those
other calls for love:
bitterness,
complaints,
fear and pain.

So when
Anger comes by,
I welcome him,
then listen to
his call for love,
lovingly.

LOST?

A friend
said "Hello" today.

As we stopped and talked,
she said, "I'm so sorry
you lost your son."

I smiled,
saying,
"Thank you."

I feel
warmed,
cared for
when someone
remembers you,
Derek,
and says
your name.

Then I thought:

I miss you
more than
words can say,

but the word *lost*

doesn't fit.

You
were never
lost in life.
Why would we
think of you
as lost now?

HILLSIDE ROCK

Between garden and sea,
a rock outcropping,
a madonna and child.

Nature-sculpted cliffs
on wooded hillside
bless his grave.

At times,
I forget him
for a while;

it's then I realize
she's still there
in prayer.

EACH TIME

Plane lifts into sky.
Your message to Dawna
encircles me,
assures me.

"Don't be afraid to fly.
I'm flying with you."
Encircling me.
Touching me.

I am blessed.
An angel's hand,
a soul across time
warms my shoulder.

ONLY TWELVE

Remember,

childhood
is only
twelve
years
wide?

SHOW ME

Mom,
I want to know.
I need to know.

Just

show me,
show me how.

WHAT'S IMPORTANT?

Cub Scout badges
sewn on by a boy
may not be even.

A sleeping bag bed
made up by a child
may have a wrinkle.

Christmas gift aprons
sewn by youngsters
will not have a label.

Children-owned animals
may be a motley lot
cared for and loved.

Ledger and bankbook
kept by a small boy and girl
may not be bookkeeper neat.

One step to success
then another is taken;
enthusiasm builds on itself.

Salad, pasta or pie
may not be perfectly made,
yet what is really important?

FEAR AND PARENTING

Parenting is not
protecting
but
loving,
preparing
our children
to be independent,
unbound from our
limiting dreams and fears.

Free to
contribute
to our world.

Not knowing
what, where or how
that unique
contribution
will be made.

Constant
amazement
is ours,
as we
encourage
our children
to explore
with awareness.

In wonderment
we watch them grow
through their choices
and ours.

We are still learning
to ask ourselves,
"Are we saying
no or yes
because
of our fears?"

Fear
is a call for love.

Love
is letting go of fear.

Parenting
is loving
as we let go of fear.

HOW LONG?

I understand
the sight of me
brings thoughts
you find hard
to comprehend.

I see our pain.
I feel our fear.

Could it happen?

Yes, it could.
And if it did,
you would survive
and come to know
my yearning.

Please see me
as just a friend.

How long must I understand?

ONLY ONE PERSON

Only
one person
ever told me
they recognized you,
Derek, as I did.

She needed
only
four words
to tell me.

That instant bond
to another lifetime
etched in my memory.
Written in a neon tube
across a moonless midnight sky.

Now, her life
is being blessed
by your gentle mature soul.

ACROSS LIFETIMES

In awe
I watched.

I felt it;
I saw the light,
their faces, resplendent
as He confirmed
their choice.

Souls
touched –
mother and child.

It
was
months
before
I understood
the commitment
made that day.

I am privileged.
I am a witness.
Awe-filled.

CHILD LIGHT

The peace
and light of God
are shining on us now.

As I watch
our children
they too are light.

How do you touch
a moonbeam,
lightning,
a soft glow,
sunlight?

Watch, enjoy
the splendor
moving freely.

Dawna,
witty and thoughtful.
An independent moonbeam,
sparkling, laughing, dancing
across this meadow of my life.
Yet at times
a bolt of lightning,
surge of thunder,
cutting through
what stands in her way
during a disquieting storm.

Our tiny
stillborn baby,
our child unknown,
is a gentle loving glow.

Derek,
who moved
on at thirteen,
is sunlight smiling
on my meadow.
His mellow consistency
smooth,
warming,
resonant
as dawn and sunset.

The peace
and light of God
are shining in me now.

SPRING'S MIRACLE

Spring rejuvenates.

Our perception shifts.
That's a miracle.

Spring focuses on the *now*.

Flowers,
leaves,
the songs of birds
all burst forth
with the joy of this moment.

Spring sings, "Remember."

"Look,
feel,
remember.
Memories are part
of who we are today."

Spring eloquently touches me.

It helps me
reach out in love,
even when I'm hurting.
Sharing love and caring
softens my pain,
brings joy
and courage to others.

Spring gives life to what looked dead.

Life was there
though unseen
in leafless
trees.

Spring brings a timeless cycle of renewal.

It lets me know
that life goes on
for those we love
but cannot see.

LIFE'S STREAM

My stream
of life began,
soft, drizzle-soaked,
grass-covered slopes.

As a thin rivulet,
glistening in the sun,
I wandered down the hillside.

Flowing,
flattened
into puddles,
resting, growing
before moving on.

Youth,
my rainy season,
unbounded
exploration
was all right
as long as I
honored the laws
of the universe.

Racing
down rapids,
around boulders,
riding white water,
leaping over waterfalls
with fearless, endless energy.

Joy in leaping.
Pain in falling.
There was no time
for backwaters or eddies
when I could shoot rapids.

The uneven
rhythm of youth
pulled me on my way
into the mainstream,
cutting into the brae.

I carved cliffs,
flooded fields,
ripped out
fences.

Misjudgments,
yes, yet in life
there are no isolated incidents,
no unconnected lessons.

Days,
months
and years
slip over
the spillway together.
Mistakes
are dammed up,
lessons
still unlearned.

Then
one day
I slowed.
Fascinated
by drifting clouds,
I swirled gently,
floating there
in the sun.

Learning to flow,
minimizing friction,
I flowed
over and around
rocks and trees
along my banks
within my path.

Sharing,
merging with
those who
came to meet me.
I reached toward
some currents gently,
enfolded others
longingly,
lingered,
loved.

At times,
I held on
in brackish
backwater
a moment,
then let go,
recalling
holding on
causes blockage
and often pain
for all involved.

Accepting what came,
you and I, my friends,
flowed together
then apart.

I am with you
gently now
as far as you
allow my strength,
my current,
to go with you.

Please use
your current
to carry me
when I need rest,

    or

you may
leave me
for a while
as you flow on

    or

race
past me
to the sea,
having learned
this life's lessons
more quickly than I.

I will

slowly,

maybe painfully,

fill the space you left.

Here
I must
recall
no life,
no water,
no matter
are ever lost.

When I have gone
as far as I can go,
quietly I will wait
for the renewing current
of life's next experience.

My stream
merging with others
becomes a family of streams,
a wide meandering river.

River
deepens,
continues
calmly with purpose,
flows gently, modestly,
with growing humility,
maturity.

The ocean
ultimately calls
my stream, my soul.

Will my river water
evaporate to clouds,

to rain,
another lifetime?

RESERVATIONS

Living,
we soon forget
God has only
lent us
to this world.

Our sons,
our daughters,
in fact all of us,
come with reservations
for our flight
to another experience.

No one-way tickets are issued.

TO ANOTHER MOTHER

Growing through our pain may be
the most courageous thing
we ever do.

Some things are
as clear
as rain-washed air
to me,
strange
as they may seem
to you.

That's all right.

We each choose
our own path
through
grief.

Reaching out
to you
helps me.
I hope
it will
help you.

LIFE'S SCHOOL

Were the world
a perfect place,
where would my soul
go to school?

This community
we call our earth
holds relationships
and experiences
from which I learn.

Are we in this world confused
as to why we're here?
We cry, hide or scream,
calling out for the love
we must learn to give.

As we learn to live and be,
why is it so hard to see
each other and ourselves
as God sees you and me,
created perfectly?

It seems this life
we've known
is a grade
in school.

HOMEWORK

My soul has homework.
What must I learn today?
Lessons toward enlightenment
often come in strange ways.

I know I am part of the peace,
the light that's here.
Yet I ignore it, crumple it,
even start to toss it away,
then ask, "When will it come?"

Down deep, I know the peace;
the light is here today.
I trap it in limited vision.
I refuse to see my illusion.

Like the tree I think I see,
then chemistry shows it
again multidimensionally
in elements and atoms.

Who is the teacher?

It's you.   It's me.

QUICK OR LINGER

It seems to me
death has two doors:
"Quick" and "Linger."

"Before we die
God pauses for
a talk with us.

Together
the choice is made
of the door
through which we pass.

"Quick"

   or

"Linger"

  not

how
or when
or where.

No matter which
door we choose,
we leave this body.
It's no more than
clothing that we wear.

To exit quickly
is the choice
some people make.
Especially
those who live
in clear, crisp
relationships.

They have no need
to be here longer.

They know
those they leave
are strong enough
to stay and learn
without them here.

Quick death
may be violent.

In time we see
a gentle beauty,
grace and freedom
in this choice.

Go quickly.

Some souls
turn before they come
through this life's door.
They choose not to enroll.

A stillborn baby
may only
need the time
he stayed within
his mother's womb.

Was something
rebalanced
or completed
for his soul?

As resolution came,
he was free
to then move on
to touch
the lives of others.

My friend
chose to take
his own life.
He showed me that
reliefless anguish,
possibly poor choices
and endless inner strife
brought a restlessness
for a new beginning.

It was an anxious
call for the love
we each ultimately
discover within.

I see him
as a soul
now freed.
Another chance.

He'll re-enroll
to once again
begin learning
unlearned lessons.

A redesigned curriculum
with possibly a slower,
less ambitious pace
toward eternal peace.

Some of us choose
the door marked
"Linger."

We need to go slowly,
lingering for a while.

Often an illness
gives us time to
resolve relationships,
express feelings,
release those loved,
help others learn
to let go.

As we learn and grow
towards commencement,
often called death,
peace may come.

There are
lessons for all of us
while our lives touch.

It helps me
to remember
God asks us,
"Are you ready to graduate?"

      or

"Is there a need to stay awhile?"

He reminds us
that in lingering
we slow the growth
of others and ourselves.

It so often seems
the gentle souls go first,
the ones we think
our world needs most.

We must remember
they have learned
their lessons
well enough to graduate.

It is those who stay and cry
who need to realize
that we are here
because we have
more lessons
still to learn.

They,
He,
you and I
are ever one.

WOVEN

Our life
a woven
free-form
fabric sculpture.

Each
strand,
twist,
texture,
color,
unique.

Families
are organic,
ever-changing weavings.

Ours was a closely woven piece,
blue, purple, pink and turquoise
flares and flashes of brilliant color.

One day

the turquoise
strand –
we knew,
    loved,
       had grown
to depend upon,
was suddenly

              jerked out,
                                        torn off.

Extracted from the weaving dream.

Three
strands
continue
the sculpture
instead of four.

At each
point of contact
where the turquoise
would have touched
the purple,
    blue
  and
pink – maturing to rose,
the weaving pattern changes.

The strand
against which
it was to weave
must make another choice –
leave a gap or weave closely.

At first our weaving
shuttled faster than before,
with the events
and decisions
made together.

Then
our weaving
lost its rhythm

gaping

                    holes

sag_{ged}
          in   sadness.

The weaving weakened.

Three braid,
two twist
as one stands apart
and feels alone
where four wove easily.

Now,
tighter
once again –
maybe even
tighter than before.
Its twisted
     braided
     woven shape
much altered from before.

Tears and time,
light's understanding,
have washed each strand
a more gentle,
less brashly
vivid hue

still woven.

MY NOTEBOOK

As a child
it lets me
be a mother.
It's part of me.
I hold it
on my lap, in my arms,
or it sits beside me.

As a friend,
like no one else,
it says the name
back to me
I long to hear.
It lets me
talk, cry or laugh,
then cry, again and again
if I feel the need.
It doesn't leave
as Derek did.

As a teacher
it lets me
look, feel, then grow
into a new freedom
with and from
the past.

My notebook
absorbs my anguish,
      my grieving,
      my pennings,
      my trickling thoughts,
      my raging rivers of remembrance,
      my awakening awareness.

My child.
My friend.
My teacher.

I hope you have a notebook.

GOOD MORNING, SON

You died
a year
ago,
though
you're
not gone.

As Dawna says,
"Derek
is with us
wherever we go,
even when
we can't see him."

Good morning, Derek,

I need to thank you
for walking,
working,
writing,
being
with me today.

My perspective changes . . .

RESOLUTION

Did I really
want
to finish grieving?

I wasn't sure.
Yet I needed to.

As I say
good-bye,
I move anger,
sorrow – vividly
painful memories –
from foreground
into background.

Dusk moves into twilight.
Grief fades reluctantly
as does night
toward dawn.

I stroll
slowly,
carefully
across this knoll.

I resolve
to live again.

NOW

I realize
more than before

each moment,
family
and
life
are
so
fragile.

Savor today.
Smell it.
Taste it.
Touch it.
Feel.

Light it with
caring,
seeing,
being,
love.

Now will be *gone* tomorrow.

FOREVER FREE

What's left to fear?

Those who trek
in this climb
toward understanding
can sometimes accept the gift
of being forever free of fear.

We have struggled, survived, discovered
we are souls, and souls float free.

Those who have gone on
are not just the body we knew.
They, too, are more than seen.

Having grown through
the greatest fear
life offers us,

I have nothing
left to fear.

I am free.

Possibly,

forever

free.

PASTURE GATE

I
now
know
death
is a gate,
not a wall.

Today, I stood
talking with him
over our pasture gate.

It was I
who had to say it.

Derek,
"I must
let you go.
I have
weeds to hoe,
seeds to plant.
I'm needed here
in this growing garden."

His smile confirmed it.

"You finished your work here.

Ride on across the pasture.
Ride on to what you must do.
Ride on, my son.
Ride on."

An ending and a beginning
came at a pasture gate.

THREE MESSENGERS

An Easter lily,
nearly forgotten
on the porch,
sprouted,
then grew.

Months ago
the lilies
bloomed,
but this one
had something
on its mind,
a timing
all its own.

Two years ago
today
we last saw
your smile.

On the porch,
radiant
in three
full blooms,
the lily
greeted me
this

August
morning.

A NEW DAY

I need to finish grieving.

I need to say
not only
"Good morning, Son,"
but
"Good morning, World."

I have faced your death.
I talk with you.

I recognize
that part of me,
that part of you,
which float free.

When I need you near,
your advice comes clear.

I understand;
you needed to go on.
I am no longer angry
you left me here.

Finishing
doesn't mean
erasing or forgetting.

It means being freed
of that throbbing pain,
guilt, sorrow, regret
of active grieving.

Yet grief does not die.
Still I sometimes cry
with gentle, lonely pain
of missing you.

I'm still here.
I have growing,
helping yet to do.

Most often, you will find me
smiling with happiness
and warm deep joy.

I knew you,
I know you
as my son.

WADING

Wade in
living stream,
illumined peace.

Notes on resolution . . .

TO HELP ME – TO HELP YOU

At this point the reader will find a shift from the poetry. Poetically formatted prose, checklists and other self-help materials are an abrupt change, yet they are an integral part of the growth the author experienced. This collection of information was prepared for her own use and has been included in case others might find the same items helpful.

Poetically formatted prose:

OUR GOOD-BYE relates the memorial service for Derek and has been meaningful for many people who were present, as well as for those who were unable to attend this memorable experience.

HOW CAN YOU HELP? answers this frequent question. In this section, the author recalls how people helped her family as they grappled with the deaths of their two children. These pieces were included to help others see how they can be of assistance when faced with the question, "What can I do to help a grieving person or family?"

Newspaper Articles:

The reprint of two newspaper stories which appeared at the time of Derek's death gives an editor's and a news reporter's perspective of him and his family.

OUR GOOD-BYE

To help other families
understand grief,
I realized, it is important
to share your memorial service.

August 29, 1984.

We were the ones
who had to do it.
The three of us.

No one else
knew you
as we did.

We thought
we had said
"good-bye"
to you, Derek.

However,
in letting
you go in love
rather than in anger,
we found
we've said
"Hello"
to you
at each new turn,
each new day in our lives.

I know you were there that day
even though we couldn't see you.

Remember,

morning light
beamed through
the stained-glass windows,
blessed the flowers,
then flooded on to touch
each person in the church.

Mrs. Thomson,
your piano teacher,
played tenderly as they entered.
The song, 'Jesu', Joy of Man's Desiring,'
soared overhead such as
I'd never heard before.

The large church wasn't large enough.
Many stood or sat outside.

As I looked out
across that audience,
my mind registered each face.

I realized
the diversity of the world
in these friends
who had come to say
they too would miss you.

How had a boy
of thirteen years
touched so many lives?

To open the service,
the three of us stood
together in front of the altar
while your Dad prayerfully read
the thoughts
the three of us had shared
earlier that morning,
the fifth day
after
you died.

It's a prayer worth remembering.

"Dear Father,

We join together in memory of Derek
and of all others who have passed
from this physical existence.

Our family feels
Your comfort and Your love,
which have been so freely expressed
to us from around the world.

We pray
that our friends who mourn today
might feel that same comfort.

Please hold
them in Your arms, Lord.
Heal them of grief,
sorrow, anger, fear and regret.

Our faith in You is our strength.
All is well with You at our side.

Through this experience of losing a child,
help us all find Your gifts
of joy, peace, love, hope and rest.

Lead us into new pastures of awareness,
nourish us with the full dimension of
Your spirit
so we can each renew
our commitment
to life.

Amen."

Suzan Boatman
walked forward to sing
'You'll Never Walk Alone'

It was the song Auntie Pat
had sung at our wedding
as Dad and I began our walk
in life together.

It's a song the four of us,
you and Dawna, Dad and I,
sang often.

'You'll Never Walk Alone'

When you walk through a storm,
hold your head up high,
and don't be afraid of the dark.
At the end of the storm is a golden sky
and the sweet silver song of a lark.

Walk on through the wind,
walk on through the rain,
though your dreams be tossed and blown.
Walk on, walk on, with hope in your heart
and you'll never walk alone.
You'll never walk alone.

Uncle Patt
stood next to speak.

You were going to spend
a week's vacation with him at the ranch
when the collision occurred.

He mentioned
that his heart went out especially
to the young men and women, your peers,
who were struggling to accept your death.

As he reached out to comfort others,
their hearts went out to him.

"Derek had an uncanny ability
to be friends with people of all ages.
One of his very special friends
was his grandmother.
They spent hours,
literally weeks, working
in the garden together.
Derek understood how
to help things grow.

See acknowledgment on page 268.

Another special friend was Rebecca,
a little girl, one year old.
When you saw
the two of them together,
their eyes were lit with joy.

Derek had the ability
to be friends with
all of us,
all ages.

Like myself,
I see men out there
who saw Derek as their own son.

I feel a great gratitude
in my heart towards
Bill, Phyllis and Dawna
for sharing Derek
with us
in a way that was
so open and free.

Sharing a child
makes them somehow bigger;
they have more and more love to give.

Derek grew like that.
He affected all of us.
Everyone who ever knew him,
even knew him for a short time,
seemed to remember him.

People who saw him years ago,
working with me in the mountains,
will stop even now and ask me,
'How's your little nephew?'
I tell them:
'He's not so little anymore.
He's growing like a weed.
He's just as nice.'

Derek had
a wisdom about him.
We all recognized this quality in him.
It was a quiet wisdom.

There is a story I'd like to tell:

One time
Phyllis ran a red light.
Derek was in the back seat.
He was barely two years old.
Just beginning to talk.
Phyllis was busy driving along.
She didn't noticed
a policeman had pulled up behind her.
The lights were flashing,
but the siren wasn't on.
Derek reached up
and tapped her
shoulder.

'Mom, I think you have a problem.'

Derek's
gentle countenance
will stand close to us,
will live with all of us forever.

There is a poem
I would like to read.
It says the author is unknown.
But I suppose that after you have read it once,
you will know the heart of its author very well.
You probably know him or her
as well as anyone can know another person.

Let me read it:

'A Child is Loaned'

' *I'll lend you for a little time*
a child of mine,

See acknowledgment on page 268.

He said.
For you to love the while he lives
and mourn for when he's dead.
It may be six or seven years,
or thirty-two or three,
But will you, till I call him back,
take care of him for me?
He'll bring his charms to gladden you.
Should his stay be brief,
you'll have his lovely memories
as solace for your grief.
I cannot promise he will stay,
since all from earth return.
There are lessons taught
I want this child to learn.
I've looked this wide world over
in my search for teachers true
From the throngs that crowd life's lanes,
I have selected you.'

He selected Bill, Phyllis and every one of you.

'Now will you give him all your love,
nor think the labor vain.
when I come to call
and take him back again?
I fancied that I heard them say,

"Dear Lord, Thy will be done.
For all the joy Thy child shall bring,
the risk of grief we'll run.
We'll shelter him with tenderness,
we'll love him while we may.
And for all the happiness we've known,
forever grateful stay.
Should the angels call for him
much sooner than we've planned,
we'll brave the bitter grief that comes,
and try to understand." ' "

After Uncle Patt finished,

your sister,
Dawna,

with remarkable poise,
composure that belied her 15 years,
walked to the lectern and shared.

" 'Simple Gifts' was a very special song
to Derek and me.

In a lot of ways
Derek was so simple;
he had enough of everything
and more to share with everyone else.

He sang the solo in this song
with his junior high school choir this spring.

I'd like to share the words with you:

'Tis a gift to be simple.
'Tis a gift to be free.
'Tis a gift to be gentle.
'Tis a gift to be fair.
'Tis a gift to wake
and breathe the morning air.
And every day to walk
in the path we choose
is a gift we pray
we may never
come to lose."

She then walked to where the choir was standing.

The choir loft was filled to overflowing
with your friends from school, Derek.

They sang the song again, for you.

This time
it was Dawna
who stepped out
in front of the choir
and sang your solo.

'Simple Gifts'

'Tis a gift to be simple.
'Tis a gift to be free.
'Tis a gift to come down where we ought to be.
And when we find ourselves in the place just right,
we'll be in the valley of love and delight.

When true simplicity is gained,
to bow and to bend we shan't be ashamed.
To turn, turn will be our delight,
'til by turning, turning
we come 'round right.

'Tis a gift to be gentle.
'Tis a gift to be fair.
'Tis a gift to wake and breathe the morning air.
And every day to walk in the path we choose
is the gift that we pray we may ne'er come to lose.

'Tis a gift to be simple.
'Tis a gift to be free, free, free.

Traditional Shaker Hymn

Your Dad
then walked to the lectern.

"It's a gift to be free.
That's the relationship
I tried to have with Derek.
I didn't want him to take hold
of my fears and prejudices.

I wanted him to be free.
Free to move well beyond . . .

Three things come to mind
that I want to share with you,
because there are so many lessons
I learned from him.
I just can't hold them back.
They need to be shared.

I worked with him in conquering fear . . .
I saw him conquer more fear than I could conquer.

When we first moved to our property,
Derek was five years old.
There was a clump of trees, kind of a thicket.
He was afraid to go down there,
even in the daylight.

It wasn't long before
he had cleared the whole thicket.

I still remember the last time he reached for my hand.

Many of you parents
will also remember that special moment.
You soon realize that a milestone has passed.
You wait for the next time
they reach for your hand,
but it doesn't happen
again.

I remember that time.

The picture of Derek on the Memorial Card
is one I took at Machu Picchu in Peru.
I really took the picture
because I wanted to remember the stairs
as they had been carved into the Inca Trail.
I asked him to sit on the rock.
I didn't realize why
I was taking
the picture.

Last April,
hiking from
the Inca ruins of Machu Picchu,
Derek wanted to explore all of the trails.

One trail was sufficiently dangerous,
the group had been cautioned not to climb it.
You can guess whose fear kept us
from climbing that trail.
It wasn't Derek's, it was mine.
We climbed the easy trails.
That's where I took the picture
that you are holding in your hand.

I watched Derek develop love.
I don't know that I helped him.
He did that himself.

He loved all the animals at the place, each one.

I can't tell you
how much he loved his friends in 4-H.
Many of you were with him two weeks ago
as you stayed with your animals
at the county fair.

He loved each person in his family.

He loved music.

Occasionally, I'd take him
to barbershop chorus practice.
One of the last songs we were learning
was one the Pacific Express Quartet sings,
*'Everybody Wants To Go To Heaven
But Nobody Wants To Die'*
He sang lead in that song.

He loved dancing, riding,
sharing his experiences
with all of us.

The joy of this last summer
was beyond what we had ever known.

That's why we feel that his time had come.

I don't think he had a sad moment
this whole past summer.
He did everything
he wanted to do.

The third thing I want to share
is that he had hopes.

He had overcome a fear of flying
and was anxious to become a pilot
as soon as he was old enough.

He long ago learned to drive
and drove his old pickup
all over the property.
It seemed a long time
before he would be

   sixteen.
Old enough for a
driver's license.

We were starting to think of a motorcycle trip
across Australia in about two years.
The trip I had taken years ago.

He couldn't wait to buy a horse for roping.

He was anxious to continue with music –
piano, oboe and singing –
expressing himself
in those ways.

And . . .
I can never remember a time
when I did something for him
that he didn't say "thank you,"
no matter how small.

I can't say the same thing.

My hope for all of you is –
    That you can conquer fear.
    That this experience
        may help you conquer fears.
    That you can develop love.
        I know you have
        because we have felt it.
        We feel it now.
    That you have hopes.
    That this be the first day
        of the rest of your life.

The trip to Peru
was with people interested
in an organization called WORLD NEIGHBORS.

Bill and Lila Yeager were
with us on that trip
and are here today.
We have asked
Bill to share."

Bill walked to the lectern.

"All of us on the trip to Peru were there to see
the results of WORLD NEIGHBORS' efforts
in that area of the world.

We are an organization
of concerned people,
helping people
learn to help
themselves.

As we met Derek,
the first word that came to our minds
was that he seemed to be such a 'shining' person.

It was interesting to see
how comfortable he was with adults.
The two Davies youngsters
were the only children on the trip.
They both fit in very quickly.

He seemed to love nature
and the out-of-doors.
He went out of his way
to be friendly and helpful.

The most memorable part
of the trip was the Altiplano.
This high country is very remote.
The roads were extremely steep and treacherous.
It seemed we were getting out of the bus constantly
to push out of the ruts and mud ponds that formed
in the road during the rainy season that had just passed.

The most exciting part of the whole trip
was to see what had actually happened
in the villages where WORLD NEIGHBORS
had been assisting.
In one of these remote high communities
at about 14,000 feet in elevation,
in an effort
to thank us
for the changes
that had occurred,
the villagers met us
in traditional costumes
with dancers and musicians.

We followed them along a little path.
They showed us the increased crops,
their experimental plots
and their improved livestock.
At the community hut we saw
the handcrafts the women had made.
They showed us the ways
in which nutrition, sanitation and health
of the people in the village improved since
WORLD NEIGHBORS had come to help them.

Derek had brought one of his ropes along.
On the way back to the bus
I watched him show the villagers
some tricks with the rope
to everyone's delight.

Another memorable moment was when
the chiefs and mayor
of an adjoining village
came to ask WORLD NEIGHBORS
to come to their village
and help them accomplish
the same improvements
they had been watching occur
in the neighboring community.

These people
were discovering
what Derek already
knew about life and agriculture.

There is great value
in gentle loving care,
in the helping of people,
in the care of land,
in the opportunity
to introduce them
to appropriate technology,
which helps them learn
to experience success.

Derek understood agriculture
because that was his industry.

He paid his own way on that trip.
That would not have been possible
had it not been for his
and his sister's enterprising efforts.

In that regard we have much in common.
WORLD NEIGHBORS' goal is not to help people,
but help them discover the thrill of success
as they learn how to solve their own problems.

Later today we will pick up our lives.
We are going to go back to doing
our own thing, in our own way.
But we will take Derek's light
and example with us,
in our minds,
in our hearts.

He knew,
he always knew
there was work to do,
some of it God's work.
He knew that there were
many truths to be discovered,
that there were many to befriend,
few to serve.

And so be it."

For four days
there had been
so many people,
phone calls and decisions,
I had not found a quiet moment
to prepare what I would say
at your memorial service,
until after the service actually began.

Standing at the pulpit,
I was aware of the calmness,
the peace I felt – even though
I had never before spoken
to an audience of 700 people.

"There have been only two times in my life
when I have felt so held and so loved
as I have in these last few days.
I want to tell you about the other time.

It was when I was giving birth to Derek.
We chose to have no one else with us
during that process
until the very
last
moment.

Bill was with me.

I remember feeling
as if I were suspended
on a cloud of love.

I have absolutely no recollection of pain,
with no medication –
just hard work,
joy and love.

That is what I have felt these days,

because you
and other friends
all around the world
have heard of Derek's death,
have come, have cared, have called
or sent your prayers
to support us.

I want to thank you all
from the bottom of my heart
for letting me experience this one more time.

I feel very privileged
to have known Derek
as well and
for as long
as I knew him.

We lived life very fully.
We have no regrets.

Each of you knew Derek in some special way,
because Derek was somehow able to meet
each of us where we were
and experience life
in the dimensions that we understood.
He rarely imposed another side of himself on us.

Those of you who heard him sing, or sang with him,
never saw him milk at 4:30 in the morning
when it was cold and dark.

He didn't like the dark.

He went out there anyway.
He never once ever said,
'I don't want to do chores.'

That issue never came up.

Those animals needed care.
It was Derek's time to do it.

People who
saw him western dance,
except for Dawna and me,
never saw him milk.

You who danced with him,
or whom he taught how to dance,
may not have seen him in school
where he was on the Honor Roll.

Some of you attended our goals class
the four of us occasionally taught,
called "Living Intentionally."
Derek knew how to do that
very, very well.

Some of you knew him as a businessman.
Let me tell you, he watched his pennies.
Those of you who bought eggs from him,
beef, something from the garden,
or had dealings with him
in his investment program with real estate,
never saw him rope.

Derek,
in his
thirteen years
of living with us,
lived more
than many people
live in a lifetime.

He was always smiling.

More than any other comment
that people made about him to me
has been regarding his smile.

He always seemed to be happy.

You know,
most of all,
he always knew
where he was needed.

I am extremely clear
Derek was needed on that airplane.

He was the happiest kid in the whole world
when I hugged him good-bye and waved
as he got on that airplane.

He was going to the ranch.
He was going to get to rope.

He wouldn't have to rope on foot anymore.

He had been out there chasing the lambs.
He gave up on the cattle because
they got smart after awhile
and could get away from him.
If he could get the lambs
in a small enough area,
he could catch them on foot.

When all else failed,
he would rope
the sawhorse.

The last things
Derek put in his suitcase
were his ropes
and a book.

A book called 'Why We Win.'
It was written by the
1981 World's Champion Team Roper,
Walt Woodard.

Walt came today
to share with you
the Derek that he knew."

Walt speaks of his experiences last spring.

"I knew Derek a lot different than most of you did.

He came to a Roping School that I had.

His mother
was working
the catch pen,
taking off ropes.

I thought that
it would be fun for Derek to catch,
then go down and visit with his mother.

But the one thing Derek
had to do was catch a steer.

I thought,
'That's going to be my goal while I'm here.
I want that boy to catch a steer by one foot,
then go down there and have a celebration
with his mother.'

But when he rode into that arena
on a horse that he had borrowed
from Alex Madonna,
his stirrups were too long;
he was bouncing.

I thought, 'Oh, my God.'

He listened to what I said
and followed the words
right to the note.
He improved.

I thought, 'If he can't ride well,
it's going to be tough.'

The first night he did well;
the next night he did a little better.
He heard some mention of a jackpot
with all the students
the last night.

He asked me if anybody could get in the contest.

I thought, 'Son!'

But said,
'All you need is a dollar and a big heart.'
He had a big heart.
He got in the contest.
I was hoping
he would catch the first one
and go down to that catch pen.

He caught the first one.
He went down to the catch pen.
I thought, 'Now that's one.'

His mother took his rope
off the steer's leg.

He came back, and he caught the next steer.
He made it to the finals.
It was a three-steer contest.

The last steer.
I thought, 'There's just no way.'
He roped the steer, and he won the contest.

When he did,
the first thing
that came to my mind was
'God, what a teacher I am!'

I know
that I've said
the same things
to 500 kids every year,
but not one of them has ever done what he did.

I'll always remember the heart that he had,
the things that he accomplished
and that smile.

When they came and told me
that the plane had crashed,
I thought of something I had heard.
'We all came from somewhere,
and we're going someplace.'

The builder of the universe
didn't create this as a stairway to nowhere.

I'll see him someday. I'll be there.
I hope he doesn't keep practicing,
because when I get there
I'll be in trouble."

Then
Bill, Dawna and I
stood together and
invited everyone present
to come out to our place for lunch.
We assured them there would be plenty of food.

Bill then introduced John-David.

"John-David Webster is a special friend of ours.
He has led the music
at several CFO retreats we've attended.
We've been together singing many times."

John-David explained that the words to the songs
we would be singing were inside the Memorial Card.

He then added,
"We have all had the privilege
of knowing Derek in various ways.

If you are like me,
you've had the sense of
'I wish I had known him better.'

Indeed, we'll have that opportunity . . .

But now
we can at least know him
in the essence and spirit that were his.
These songs were selected with that in mind.

That we might know him and experience
the real essence of his philosophy,
his thinking and his spirit.

We'll begin with the first song."

'Life is for Living'

Life is for living,
  whatever you will live for
  you will give.
Life is for giving,
  whatever you will give
  to life will live.
Life is for doing,
  for living, giving, doing,
  learning how.
Life is for you,
  and life is for me.
Life is for living now!

Life is for loving,
  whatever you will love
  enough is yours.
Life is for sharing,
  whatever you will share
  with others grows.
Life is for being,
  for loving, sharing, being,
  learning how.
Life is for you,
  and life is for me.
Life is for living now!
Life is for living now!

See acknowledgment on page 268.

"They wanted you to have these songs,
in your hearts and minds.
Now that you've had a chance to rehearse,
let me really see and hear you
sing it like you mean it."

It was sung with gusto
the second time,
Derek.

'Freely, freely you have received. Freely, freely give.'

'Freely, Freely'

God gave me love in Jesus' name*
I've been born in Jesus' name
And in Jesus' name I come to you
To share His love
as He told me to.

He said,
'Freely, freely you have received,
Freely, freely give.
Go in my name
and because you believe,
others will know that I live.'

All power is given in Jesus' name
In earth and heaven in Jesus' name
And in Jesus' name I come to you
To share His power
as He told me to.

He said,
'Freely, freely you have received.
Freely, freely give.
Go in my name
and because you believe,
others will know that I live.'

See acknowledgment on page 268.

"Bind us together,
bind us together,
with cords that cannot be broken . . .

Bind us together with love.

If you would like to, reach out and touch
someone."

Everyone joined hands.

'Bind Us Together'

Bind us together Lord,
bind us together with cords
that cannot be broken
bind us together Lord
bind us together
bind us together with love.

There is only one God
there is only one King
there is only one Body
that is why we sing.

Bind us together Lord
bind us together with cords
that cannot be broken
bind us together Lord
bind us together
bind us together with love.

"Let us conclude in that same atmosphere.

Let there be peace on earth and let
it begin with me."

See acknowledgment on page 268.

'Let There Be Peace'

Let there be Peace on Earth,
And let it begin with me.
Let there be Peace on Earth,
The peace that was meant to be.
With God as our Father,
Family all are we.
Let us walk with each other,
In perfect Harmony.
Let Peace begin with me,
Let this be the moment now.
With every breath I take,
Let this be my joyful vow –
To take each moment
and live each moment
in peace eternally.
Let there be Peace on Earth,
and let it begin with me.

Amen

We invited
everyone again.
"Please come for lunch,
we need each one of you."

The TV news that evening reported that
between 300 and 400 people came to share
in the abundant food and visiting at our place.

Derek,
the memorial service
is how we thought we had said "good-bye."

See acknowledgment on page 268.

Derek 'had already lived a lifetime'

By Susan Seager
Staff Writer

At 13, Derek Davies already had a very definite course mapped out for his life.

The San Luis Obispo boy's goals for 1984 were to grow 4 inches taller, buy a home computer and a horse, learn to rope, get good grades and create "a calm, inspiring atmosphere" at home, according to a page-long list he made every year.

A more distant goal was to parlay the 12 head of cattle he owned with his 15-year-old sister, Dawna, into a ranch of his own.

But shortly after he got on Wings West Flight 628 Friday morning, Derek's goals were cut short when the passenger airplane collided with a small private plane. Derek was killed together with the 12 other passengers, two crewmen and two men flying the single-engine plane.

Phyllis and William Davies lost their only son in that crash just 10 miles from their 10-acre ranch; Dawna lost her only brother, only sibling and best friend.

Between answering phone calls from friends and relatives, the three Davies sat in their comfortably furnished mobile home and talked about the blond, blue-eyed teen-ager who seemed to be filled with endless energy.

Two days after hearing the news of his death, the closely knit, religious family is teary but calm.

"Not one of us has a regret," said Phyllis. "Derek lived a very, very full life. Most people, in their full lives, don't do as much. ... He had already lived a lifetime."

Derek smiled often but was quiet and wise, his mother said. "It's as if I raised my grandfather," said Phyllis in a soft voice. "You just can't be sad (if) you knew him."

To hear his family tell it, Derek never had a wasted, idle moment.

On the last day of his life, Derek was on his way to visit his two uncles on their ranch in rugged Alturas where he hoped to practice his newly learned skill of roping.

"There never was a boy who was so excited to get on that plane," said Phyllis.

"He loved to fly."

Tragically, Phyllis had made a reservation for Derek on an earlier flight, but had decided against putting him on that flight because he needed his sleep and more time to pack.

But Phyllis said there was a finality to Derek's leaving that she has only begun to understand. He wrote thank-you notes to those who helped him at the county fair, where he showed his prize-winning pigs with the Edna Valley 4-H Club. The notes should arrive in the mail today, she said. He also cleaned up his room and vacuumed the house, even though it wasn't his turn.

And he only gave his mother enough money for three tickets to a barbecue all four Davies planned to attend. "He should have given me $24, but he only gave me $20," she said.

Derek Davies

Derek had worked hard all summer, milking his cows and goats, making and selling goat cheese and saving his earnings. He sold one of the pigs, the 220-pound Zardeo, for about $580 at the close of the fair.

He had paid for his Wings West ticket himself, drawing from his ample bank account.

He was hoping to shine up his newly learned roping skills at his uncles' ranch. He packed two ropes and a book by his hero, world champion team roper, Walt Woodard. "I bet he read that book 25 times," his mother said.

His father took him to see Woodard perform at the county fair earlier this month.

He was to return after a 10-day trip to visit his uncles and prepare to start eighth grade at Laguna Junior High School.

Derek would probably have gone to Cal Poly, his parents' alma mater, Phyllis said.

He played the oboe and piano, and sometimes sang solos for the Laguna Junior High School choir.

Derek and Dawna shared household chores and profits from their vegetable garden and goat cheese, putting most into a savings account. Both agreed to tithe 10 percent of their earnings to the family church.

The pair, who relied on each other for friendship at their isolated home, shared a room all their lives. Now Dawna can't bear to sleep in the room alone. "She stays with us," her father said softly.

Phyllis was the last to see Derek alive. Their visit to the airport remains clearly etched in her mind. As her son stood to board the plane, Phyllis hugged him and asked for a kiss. "He said, 'Oh no, not here Mom,' and he gave me another hug," she recalled. "Then he walked toward the gate with a big smile. He turned and waved to me," she continued, her voice slightly broken.

"Father Al (Simon of the Old Mission Church) said, 'And he was already flying.' "

Memorial services for Derek will be held at 11 a.m. Wednesday at the United Methodist Church in San Luis Obispo. The Davies family will officiate.

Members of the San Luis Obispo High School and Laguna Junior High School are invited to come and sing.

Derek's cremated remains will be scattered over the family ranch.

Donations may be sent to World Neighbors, 5116 N. Portland Ave., Oklahoma City, Oklahoma 73112.

In addition his sister, Dawna, and parents, Phyllis and William Davies, Derek is survived by two uncles, Patrick Armstrong of Bishop, and Wesley Armstrong of Alturas; one aunt, Patricia Norris of East Windsor, N.J.; four grandparents, Philip and Jeannette Armstrong of San Luis Obispo, Ione Davies Isham of San Luis Obispo and Glenn Davies of Camarillo.

See acknowledgment on page 268.

Editor's Report
By Michael Wecksler

I was sitting on my porch Sunday afternoon, reading the paper and watching the cumulus clouds roll overhead. It had rained the night before, and the smell, and the feel of the air made me think it would rain again.

I was glancing at the front page when my eye caught a story about a plane wreck in San Luis Obispo, which I consider my home town.

I read the story quickly, hoping not to find a familiar name, but I did.

It hit me like an electrical shock; young Derek Davies had died in the plane wreck.

I hadn't known Derek long, but I knew him well.

I lived in a trailer for over a year on the Davies' farm. I helped milk the cows, feed the chickens and till the garden. Once I even helped cowboy-Derek rope his silly dog Skipper.

Derek and I played together, and worked together every day. Sometimes we hunted crawdads in the creek, once or twice we rode our bicycles to the beach; in short we were buddies.

I called him "Sprout" – from the Jolly Green Giant commercial I guess – and it seemed appropriate; it was only a matter of time until he would sprout into a fine young man.

At 12 he could do the work of a grown man, and he knew things that take most of us many years to learn.

In fact, Derek was such a precocious child I often wondered who was the adult in our relationship. I finally figured out it was him.

I hadn't seen Derek in over a year; once I left the farm I never visited again. I ran into his mother in San Luis Obispo from time to time, and she would tell me to go and see the kids, Derek and his sister Dawna. She told me how much they missed me, and they wanted me to visit, but I never found the time.

I guess that's the point of all this; I wish I had seen Derek at least one more time.

Most of us are pretty busy. It's easy to get tied up with your family and career, it's not always easy to keep up with friends, but we should try.

We live in a world where there are no set answers, no guarantees, and at any moment things can change drastically, as they have for the Davies family.

In one of his songs James Taylor sings "shower the people you love with love." What he's saying is if you care about someone let him know.

The world wouldn't change if I had seen Derek one more time, he'd still be dead, and I'd still be 500 miles away, thinking of him.

But if I had seen Sprout one more time I would feel a heck of a lot better today.

See acknowledgment on page 268.

HOW CAN YOU HELP?

What is helpful in grief? Though I cannot speak for other families, I can tell you what was helpful and meaningful to me and to our family.

As I look back across this period of time, an increasing number of thought-filled and casual actions – even awkward moments – warmingly come to mind. IT 'S OK TO ASK and TWO LONG WALKS relate some of these experiences. I have made an effort to thank those who helped us. However, this gives me another opportunity to say thank you. You may be surprised to find yourself in this nameless list.

You will find blank pages are included to jot notes on ideas which occur to you. These pages may be helpful personally and as you reach out to assist others.

IT'S OK TO ASK

It did
throw me off
at first
when people asked,

"How are you doing?"

"I don't know.
I'm still alive,
I guess."

Now
I cherish
"How are you doing?"
followed by
a pause.

They listen.

It tells me
someone cares,
still remembers him.

"How are you doing?"
then
listening.

Your
listening
brings relief,
a warm, grateful
smile slips across my face,
into my life.

TWO LONG WALKS

Our two walks
along grief's way
have great contrast . . .

When our
first son died,
not a single card.
Outside the family,
not even the doctor or a nurse.
No one said, "I'm sorry.
             I know it hurts
             to lose a child."

Young,
in a city,
working and in school,
less faith in God.

That time
we walked and cried
along the road of grief, alone.

When Derek died,
people in our small town
and from across the world
reached out to us with
"I need to help you if I can.
I'm hurting too."

Each tear,
each prayer,
each thought-filled
letter,
poem,
song,
card,
plant,
flower,
phone call,
dish of food . . .

people
who found the courage
to drive out and see us,
willing to risk
emotions they would face . . .

each was important.
Each is remembered:

A young man
we barely knew
came out our long dirt road,
not knowing what he would find,
knowing only that he needed to come.
He looked alone and scared,
a bunch of home-grown roses
clutched in his fist as he approached.
He recalled he had talked with Derek only once.
After a comforting visit,
he left with a smile on his face.
He had new understanding of himself,
his own courage, and grief.

The 4-H Club
came out
the day before
the memorial service.
A giant vacuum cleaner
swept over the farm.
Children, teens and parents
with rakes, pitchforks and brooms,
cleaned corrals, barn, shed, water troughs;
picked produce, weeded gardens, and mowed lawns.
They brought dinner – hot dogs, buns and marshmallows –
to cook over a campfire.

Each was important.
Each is remembered:

Those who found the time
to come to the memorial service,
to share in lunch after the service.

My mind, like a camera,
took a picture of each person.
It was then I discovered
it is more important than I ever dreamed
to attend services.

The spotless kitchen
greeted me
as I went into the house
late that afternoon
after all those friends
who came had been amply fed.

A farmer we'd never met
sent $50 with his card:
"There will be unexpected expenses.
I know, I lost my wife."

The waitress
who, in her pain,
called me Derek.
I thanked her.
"It feels so good to know you remember."

Each is remembered:

Concerts,
performances,
the 4-H yearbook
were dedicated in memory of Derek.

Editorials,
Letters to the Editor,
people from across the country
sent us news stories that mentioned him.

Peace Corps friends
heard his name on a radio
in the heart of Africa,
then walked all day to call.

Several people
called and asked, "How can I help?"
Each came out, and as we visited
they helped me clean cupboards,
                    closets,
                    windows,
          straighten the books,
               weed the garden,
                  pick produce
                  and can.

Two mothers
I had seen in town
and at school functions phoned.
"Would you like help decorating?"
For that holiday I couldn't face!
Our home had never looked "so like Christmas."
We used the favorite family ornaments,
lots of ribbon, lights, and angels.

Derek's friends
wrote letters and poems,
then gave them to us in a book.

A friend asked me
to break her colt –
that filly filled
a corner of the void.

A man who had
also lost a son
reached out and touched
Bill's shoulder as if to say,
"I know it's hard, but you'll make it."

Each is remembered:

A student from Somalia,
studying at the university,
scaled these peaks of grief
eight times in his few years.
He and his mother faced the death
of his seven brothers and his father.
He called us at least twice a month
to see how we were doing and to let us know
he was keeping us in his prayers to Allah.

A Quechua Indian family
in the mountains of Peru
sent us
a tiny braided cross.

Gifts to Dawna –
a cuddly bunny,
a soft doll
to carry,
to hold.

A young couple
gently reminded us
of Kahlil Gibran's
wise thoughts on parenting:
Children are not yours.
Parents are bows from
which arrows are sent.

The food brought
on disposable plates,
as well as
the food that came in dishes
with the sender's name
marked on the bottom and
which needed to be returned –
a visit that got me out of the house.

Those calls,
the thoughtful notes
on the anniversary of Derek's death,
on his birthday
to let us know
others still
remember him.

Loving
blessings
seen, felt
in pain-filled and
peaceful, caring smiles.

The memorial donations
to WORLD NEIGHBORS
continue Derek's efforts
toward food, health,
and dignity for those
less fortunate.

Patient friends who
encouraged me to write,
helped me with this manuscript.

He's remembered.

Another mother
just last week
said she missed Derek.
She hugged me;
tears were
in her eyes.

The lights
each year
since his death
on the Hospice Tree –
gifts that not only help
but glimmer in his memory.

Can you imagine what it means
to have someone else say his name?

Each reached out,
each shared,
each helped bear the pain.

Each thought,
each prayer
are important –
far more
than you think.

It helped our family
when someone said,
"I care."
"I'm so sorry."
"I'm hurting too."
"My thoughts are with you."
"I've been thinking about you."
"I need to tell you I miss him."
"I've never told you,
but I remember Derek doing . . .".

How could two grief experiences
in one family be so different?

Not even one card
when our first son died –
an incomprehensible contrast.

Thank you
for walking with us
on this second climb across
the mountain range of grief.

Ideas for helping others . . .

HELPFUL REFERENCES

As the author moved through her grief and reached out to help others, she found a need for information. This appendix includes checklists and other helpful information, which she compiled for her own future use out of this experience. These lists have assisted the author and other individuals facing the need to make decisions relating to a death.

WHEN SOMEONE DIES: MY CHECKLIST

Note: *In reading and referring to this list, recall that it was developed in a small rural community where I have lived much of my life. We lived in a city when our first son was born dead. At that time none of the things on this list were done. I have never experienced a death where all items on this list were completed. Each situation is different, this list is only a general guideline.*

I   =   Immediate Family
FF =   Friends or Family

DAY ONE

I   1. If death occurred by accident or in a hospital, make organ donation or medical research decisions, if appropriate.

I   2. Sign hospital papers and release, if requested.

I   3. If death occured at home, call the doctor, hospice worker or case nurse to certify death.

I   4. Follow their directives.

See acknowledgment on page. 268.

I	5.	Authorize or decline autopsy unless one is required due to circumstances.
I	6.	Call immediate family members.
I	7.	Call clergy.
I	8.	Call attorney holding the current will.
I	9.	Ask attorney if the will contains burial instructions.
I	10.	Ask the attorney for the name of the executor. (This may be important.)
I	11.	Decide upon a mortuary.
I	12.	Give mortician the location of the deceased and a contact's phone number.
I	13.	Make an appointment with the mortician as soon as those involved in decision making can meet.
I	14.	Review questions for mortician (see page 230) before meeting with them and making decisions.
I	15.	Call close family friends.
I	16.	Ask close friends and family to be available to answer the phone and greet guests.
I or FF	17.	Start a list of all phone calls and visitors.
I or FF	18.	Request phone numbers of anyone who offers to help; get addresses if possible.
I or FF	19.	Keep a list of all food delivered, label container with name and phone number for easy return; get addresses if possible.
FF	20.	Visit the family.
FF	21.	Take a copy of this book to the family. Be sure it has a bookmark at the beginning of this section.
FF	22.	After visiting for a while, ask if you can help by answering the door and taking phone calls and be aware of other needs. Then offer to be of assistance.

I or FF   23. Keep a list of all gifts; get addresses if possible.

I   24. Immediate family and close friends should check their calendars. Consider canceling appointments coming up within the next few days.

I   25. Check calendar of the deceased and notify those individuals scheduled on it.

I or FF   26. Near the phone, keep the number of an available doctor in case someone needs medical assistance.

I   27. Be aware that everyone involved is under stress.

I   28. Be sure to eat well-balanced meals. SIT DOWN to meals regularly — even if you don't want to eat or are not hungry.

I   29. Consider taking vitamins, especially for stress.

I   30. Sleep — or at least rest — is very important!

I or FF   31. Get outside in the sunshine and fresh air. When friends come to visit, suggest taking a walk together while you talk.

DAY TWO

I   32. Review deceased's "Burial and Funeral Instructions."

I   33. Discuss with family members their expectations and strong feelings regarding burial traditions, including what they feel the deceased would have wanted.

I   34. Decide whether you want a funeral, memorial service, or no service at all.

I   35. Decide between burial and cremation.

I   36. Whom do you want to officiate at the service: clergy, family, and/or friends?

I   37. Review funeral service and/or memorial service details before meeting with mortician (see page 245).

I   38. Review personalized memorial card information (see page 236).

I   39. Decide if family prefers flowers or contributions to a charitable memorial fund, educational fund or to research.

I   40. Collect the following information, as appropriate. All or some of it will be required for burial permit, obituary notice, and in closing details of the deceased.

- full, legal name
- nickname
- religious name
- city and state of residence
- how long in state
- age
- date of birth
- place of birth
- country of citizenship
- spouse's name
- maiden name
- father's name
- father's birthplace
- mother's maiden name
- mother's birthplace
- religious affiliation
- occupation and title
- type of business
- business address and phone
- social security number
- veteran's serial number
- cause of death
- place of death
- memberships
- grade schools and high schools attended
- colleges attended
- degrees
- scholarships
- positions held in public service or in religious afiliations
- awards, honors, meritorious citations
- military service
- date of enlistment
- date of discharge
- military honors
- list of surviving immediate family members
- hobbies and special interests
- special accomplishments
- famous family members
- special wishes or charitable donations

Obituary notice: If you wish to write this notice, you will need to add only the time and location of the service to this list after you have met with the mortician.

I   41. Meet the mortician.

I   42. Discuss with your mortician the items on page 230 that are appropriate to your situation.

I   43. Allow adequate time (usually four days) when you are deciding upon time and place of the service. Points to consider in this decision:

- notification of all friends and family
- their travel time to the service site
- obituary notices take several days for publication; make sure there is at least one day between publication and the service
- time of service should be set after school hours if many youth are involved
- an 11:00 a.m. service allows more working people to attend
- a Friday or Monday service may help those who must travel from out of town
- time to design, prepare and print a personalized memorial card, if desired (see page 236)
- if the service is scheduled at a church, choose one of appropriate size and denomination
- if not a church, choose a location easy to find
- if a fraternal order will be involved in the service, request their assistance immediately

I   44. Discuss costs and set budget guidelines.

I   45. Make initial decisions regarding:

- time and place of services (to be confirmed after you meet with the mortician)
- chapel use
- personalized memorial cards
- religious service
- memorial service
- funeral
- graveside service
- casket or urn
- vault
- cemetery plot location
- headstone or marker
- endowment care of cemetery plot
- opening and closing of the grave
- floral arrangements
- memorial donations in lieu of flowers

- transportation
- funeral coach
- limousines for family members
- limousines for pallbearers
- car for transporting flowers
- pallbearers
- embalming and preparation
  - restorative art
  - make up
  - hair
  - nails
  - glasses
  - jewelry
  - religious or fraternal items
  - clothing for the deceased
- viewing the deceased
- open casket service
- visitation hours for family
- visitation hours for others
- clothing for the family
  (Purchase suits, slacks or dresses, for
  family members, if needed.)
- haircuts and appointments for family members
- taped or live music
- organist
- soloist
- audio or video recording of service
- memorial record book with guest register
- photographs of family and deceased for photo display
- acknowledgment cards
- parking facilities
- police escort and traffic control
- signing necessary papers
- obituary notices
- officiating person or persons
- Be sure to review total cost of each item and total.

Note: *Review the above decisions against budget guidelines BEFORE making final decisions and signing mortuary agreement.*

I   46. Make a list or mark an address book for notification of family, close friends and business associates.

I   47. Remember that nurses and other care-givers frequently appreciate being notified since a close relationship often evolves in cases of prolonged illness.

I   48. Delegate notification process if possible. Usually it is easier for others, rather than the immediate family, to make these calls.
- The mortician will make notification phone calls, if requested to do so.
- Organizations often have phone committees, that will notify local members of a death.

I   49. When asking others to make the notification phone calls, give them brief details of the death, information about the service times and place, and memorial details.

FF   50. Make notification phone calls.

I   51. Complete the obituary notices, adding a name and phone number for additional information.

I   52. Do not place a home address in the obituary notices. Unfortunately, an announcement that the home will be vacant during the specified time of the funeral invites burglars.

I   53. Obituary notices can be delivered in person or phoned to the newspapers. Consider sending a current photo to the newspapers.

I   54. Design — or delegate the design of — memorial cards if you do not wish to use those provided by the mortuary. See page 236 for ideas and instructions.

FF   55. Make arrangements for care of children, as well as for ill or elderly immediate family.

FF   56. Make sure nutritious food will be provided for the immediate family so that no cooking will be necessary for several days.

FF   57. When people call to inquire about what food they may bring, suggest healthful casseroles, vegetable dishes, salads or fresh fruit rather than sweets and desserts.

I   58. Check with family and close friends coming from out of town to see if they need hotel accommodations or transportation. Ask a friend or other family member to assist with these details.

FF 59. Instead of saying "Call me if I can help," offer to do something specific: "Would it help if I came out and helped vacuum or wash windows while the immediate family is at the mortuary?" "Is the wood box full?" "I'm handy; does anything need to be fixed?"

I 60. People like to be given jobs to do during this time. MAKE A LIST as needs occur to you. Suggest that people who offer can be helpful by weeding the yard, cleaning the house, repairing the porch, doing the laundry, doing the chores, feeding the animals, walking pets, etc.

I 61. Some families prefer to conduct their own service. See memorial service details on page 245.

I 62. Request the assistance of clergy for the service, if desired.
   • Make appointment.
   • Gather eulogy materials, poems, stories, meaningful Scripture.
   • Favorite books of the deceased are often marked with passages that were especially meaningful and may be helpful in planning the service.
   • Recall favorite songs.
   • Meet with clergy and express preferences for the service.

I 63. Plan to limit time for service to 45 minutes.

Service can include:
• Music	as people arrive and exit
• Opening	prayer, poem, Scripture reading or statement
• Singing	solo, choral
• Service	liturgy, Mass, remembrance by family and friends
• Announcement	invitations to after-service gathering; include location or post maps at door
• Closing	songs, Scripture reading, poetry or prayers.

I 64. Consider videotaping the service. This is a *VERY* helpful grief tool for some family members and for those unable to attend the service. A professional or a friend can do this nearly unnoticed.

I   65. Consider placing pictures of the deceased in the mortuary lobby or church entry area. Often people go to a service who have had little recent contact with the family. Pictures are good updating tools when words may be difficult.

FF   66. Gather photos for display per family request.

I   67. If pallbearers are going to be used, they must be selected and notified as soon as possible.

I   68. Honorary pallbearers are an option when health precludes participation due to the lifting involved.

FF   69. Arrangements should be made for a meal after the service, if desired.

I   70. *Remember:* Friends want to help in any way they can. A potluck-style gathering is usually the easiest and provides a way for friends to assist. This also provides the grieving family with food for several days.
- Another possible solution would be to have pizza delivered. This is especially appropriate if the deceased was a young person and many youth are involved.
- Two other options are hors d'oeuvres or sandwiches.

I   71. This after-service gathering is *VERY* important because it allows friends and family to be together in a relaxed atmosphere.

FF   72. Accept after-service gathering responsibility and coordinate details.

FF   73. Offer to take food to the gathering.

FF   74. Make arrangements for a friend to housesit during the funeral to prevent theft. If theft is a likely possibility, consider using a private security agency.

I   75. Order altar flowers, casket sprays and family floral arrangements to be used during the service.

I   76. Select musicians or ask for recommendations from clergy or the mortician.

I   77. Contact musicians and ask about their fees.

I   78. Specify what music the family wishes to be used.

I   79. If the family does not know which music they want performed, give the musicians some preference guidelines. Indicate what music or songs would be unacceptable or offensive to family members.

I   80. Hire musicians.

FF   81. Offer to coordinate music details after getting cost guidelines.

DAY THREE

I   82. Finalize any remaining decisions (review item 45 in this list) with the mortician.

I   83. Review all costs.

I   84. Check and sign necessary papers.

I or FF 85. Greet and visit with friends and relatives who call.

I   86. Arrange interment or graveside services
- public or private
- with clergy and/or only with family

FF   87. At the service, a memorial record book with guest register is meaningful for most families. Offer to attend to this detail.

FF   88. Visit the family.

DAY OF THE SERVICE

FF   89. Prepare for the informal gathering after the service.

FF   90. Make sure delegated persons are at the service location early to set up and to greet early-arriving guests.

FF   91. Check to see if the family would appreciate having some of the flower arrangements delivered to hospitals, schools or care centers after the service.

FF	92.	Check to see if a map to the after-service gathering is needed.
FF	93.	As people bring food to the gathering, be sure a person is responsible for labeling dishware. This can be done on the bottom of each item with masking tape and a felt-tip pen. Label with the names and addresses of donors.
FF	94.	Buffet-style food service is easiest. Take food which can be eaten with a fork, so a knife isn't required.
FF	95.	Clean up kitchen and house after the guests leave.
FF	96.	Vacuum.
FF	97.	Freeze leftovers in meal-size packages.
I	98.	Remember to notify college and university alumni journals and associations, professional associations and organizations, and trade journals.
I	99.	Remember that many national special-interest magazines appreciate receiving — and publish — notifications.

WITHIN 3 WEEKS OF THE DEATH

I	100.	Locate and contact local grief support groups. See page 266.
FF	101.	Continue to visit or call family members.
I	102.	Make list of yet-to-be-notified persons who live out of the area. Notify them by card or letter (include memorial card).
I	103.	Prepare notice of appreciation for newspapers or arrange to use the standard formats they provide.
I or FF	104.	Make list of people to send "thank-you notes" to for flowers, calls, food and other thoughtful gestures. Purchase and help write or address the notes, if help is wanted. These notes may be printed or handwritten.
I or FF	105.	Return dishes (left after gathering) with thank-you notes.
I	106.	Obtain six (6) or more Certified Death Certificates, which are needed for official notifications, all securities transfers, as well as other proofs.

I   107. Notify landlord. Make addendum changes to rental agreements. Make moving arrangements if the person lived alone.

I   108. Notify auto/life insurance companies and file request for premium refunds.

I   109. Notify and check the following for possible benefits for survivors:
- Social Security Administration
- Veterans Administration
- Retirement fund
- Pension fund
- Life insurance
- Credit union
- Trade union

I   110. Notify and provide name changes:
- Accounts payable
  Ask for more time before payments are due, if necessary. Check on life insurance clauses that may cancel debt upon death.
- Post office and correspondents
  Send cards provided by post office.
- Bank and credit union
  Savings accounts
  Checking accounts
  Safe-deposit boxes
  Trust funds
  Money market accounts
  Credit card accounts
  IRA
- Savings & loan
  Accounts
  Loans
- County recorder
  Titles and deeds to property
- Certified financial planner
  Financial review
- Insurance
  Auto
  Health
  Personal property
  Insurance policies owned by others should be checked for beneficiary change.
- Stockbroker
  Stocks
  Bonds
  Mutual funds

- CPA
  Review tax situation
  Federal
  State
  Estate
  Inheritance
- Attorney
  Change will's beneficiary if deceased was named.
  Other will changes
- Vehicle registration
  Title
  Licensing
  Driver's license
- Utility companies
  Telephone listing
  Billing change
- Charge accounts
- Others who send bills
- Organizations
  Fraternal
  Civic
  Social

I 111. Secure home if deceased was living alone. The Police Department, if notified, will often make periodic checks on a home vacated under this circumstance.

I 112. Make appointment with attorney for reviewing will and other beneficiary matters.

I 113. Store belongings until they can be sorted.

MONTHS AFTER DEATH

I 114. Get involved in a local grief support group.

FF 115. Continue to visit or call the family occasionally.

I 116. Decide on gravestone inscription.

I 117. Check on completion date for gravestone or marker. Order it two or more months after death and arrange for placement.

I or FF 118. Make up memory book of cards and letters. In many cases this is an enjoyable and healing project that can be done alone or with a friend.

I	118.	Sorting stored belongings can be done in stages. (It has taken me three years. I'm nearly finished. There were five boxes. I sorted clothes first. Toys and books were sorted next, then the "stuff." Derek's notebooks and journals are still in storage.)

I   119.   Think in terms of five-minute blocks of time rather than in days or hours. Remember these words from page 107:

> "Five minutes:
> Dust,
> Trim a bush,
> Set the table,
> Water plants,
> Make a salad,
> Wash one window,
> Clean the bathroom,
> Straighten the living room,
> Unload–reload the dishwasher."

I   120.   If at all possible, *DO NOT* make long-term decisions regarding a move, sale of home, investments, large gifts or donations until a year or more after a death.

EVERYONE   121.   Occasionally, especially on the anniversary of death or birthday of the deceased, send an *"I've been thinking of you"* card to family members of the deceased.

EVERYONE   122.   Make an appointment with a counselor if you are struggling with grief — even years after a death. Many professionals, Hospice and other groups offer counseling to individuals and families. This can be very helpful in resolving grief and associated problems. (After seventeen years of quiet, internal grieving for our stillborn child, I finally sought help. I had not said good-bye to him because I didn't know a good-bye was needed. I wish I had known to do it sooner.)

EVERYONE   123.   *Remember:* It is *NEVER* too late to ask for professional help with your grief problems.

QUESTIONS TO ASK A MORTICIAN

Death rarely touches one's life only once. This is my personal reference list of questions for a mortician. These occurred to me or came up in conversation as I helped grieving families.

The easiest way to use this list may be to check the questions you want answered and hand it to the mortician. Request answers, comments or clarification for the marked questions. I have inserted cursory answers, which I received at various times from knowledgeable people. Your mortician or attorney will give you more explicit answers.

GENERAL INFORMATION

1. _____ What is the role of a funeral director?
    Coordinating details for the service.
    Preparing the deceased for cremation,
    burial or shipment.

2. _____ Is a funeral director available 24 hours a day?
    Yes.

3. _____ What is important in selecting a funeral director?
    Integrity, personality, facilities, proximity,
    prices.

4. _____ How soon after a death should one call a funeral director?
    As soon as possible.

ARRANGEMENTS

1. _____ Who will put the obituary notices in local newspapers?
   Immediate family or mortician.

2. _____ What information is needed for the obituary?
   See list on page 219.

3. _____ What is the role of the county coroner in a death?
   Sign death certificate in unnatural deaths.

4. _____ What is the role of the Health Department registrar?
   Register death certificate, mail copies.

5. _____ Whom should I contact to initiate insurance claims,
   Social Security, veteran's death benefits?
   *Funeral director can help you with contacts as these
   may affect service and burial arrangements.*

REQUIREMENTS

1. _____ What is an autopsy?
   Inspection by a pathologist.

2. _____ When is an autopsy required?
   Coroner may require one to determine cause of death.

3. _____ Does the law require use of a casket?
   No.

4. _____ Is it a law that remains must be embalmed?
   No.

5. _____ Why is a certified copy of the death certificate necessary?
   *For legal notification regarding insurance, stocks
   and bonds, real property and bank accounts. Also for
   claiming veteran's, Social Security and other benefits.*

LEGAL MATTERS

Note: *Consider getting legal counsel on any matters regarding a death.*

1. _____   Is a will important?
   Yes.

2. _____   Will an attorney be needed to handle the estate?
   Usually, but not always.

3. _____   How is the next of kin or executor determined?
   Check with an attorney.

PRE-NEED ARRANGEMENTS

1. _____   What is the Anatomical Gift Act?
   Body organs may be donated for transplant.
   See page 263.

2. _____   May I pay for my funeral before I die?
   Yes.

3. _____   May I make service and disposition arrangements
   before I die?
   Yes.

SERVICE ARRANGEMENTS

1. _____   Please explain the terms:
   ___ cemetery
   ___ mausoleum
   ___ crypt
   ___ niche
   ___ entombment
   ___ inurnment
   ___ urn
   ___ embalming
   ___ funeral
   ___ memorial service funeral
   ___ graveside service funeral
   ___ closed casket funeral
   ___ sealed casket funeral

2. _____   May we have a viewing, casket and funeral services
   if the body is to be cremated following these
   services?
   Yes.

3. _____   May we have a private funeral service?
   Yes.

CREMATION

1. _____   May remains be cremated in a casket?
   Yes.

2. _____   What is direct cremation?
   No services will take place.

3. _____   May a family scatter cremated remains?
   Yes.

4. _____   Are there restrictions on where remains may
   be scattered?
   Yes. Check with your mortician.

PREPARING FOR THE BURIAL

1. _____   May I have a copy of the price list
   for a funeral?
   Yes.

2. _____   Is it possible to have lodge members officiate at
   a funeral service?
   Yes.

3. _____   What are memorial cards?
   *Cards distributed at funerals and
   memorial services.*

4. _____   Who should receive thank-you cards after
   the service?
   *Persons who assisted the family and who
   sent flowers, food or memorial contributions.*

5. _____   How many pallbearers are required for a service?
   Usually six.

6. _____   May something special be placed in a casket with
   the deceased?
   Yes.

   What are the restrictions?
   Size of the casket.

7. _____   How long after death should the memorial service
   be scheduled?
   *The family decides — usually within two
   days after obituary notices appear
   in newspapers.*

8. _____   How does one ship remains to another city
   for burial?
   Ask your mortician.

AFTER FUNERAL OR MEMORIAL SERVICE

1. _____   How do I order a gravestone?
   Ask your mortician.

2. _____   What organizations exist to help with grief after
   a death?
   > *Hospice, grief support groups, churches and others are available. Ask mortician for those in your area. See page 266.*

3. _____   How do I find a private therapist?
   > *Check phone book under:*
   > > *Counselors*
   > > *Licensed Clinical Social Workers*
   > > *Psychologists*
   > > *Psychiatry*
   >
   > *Call three for a free interview appointment.*
   > *Select the one with whom you wish to work.*

Counseling is frequently much more helpful than one would expect.

Remember: It is *NEVER* too late to ask for help!

Questions I want to ask . . .

PREPARING A PERSONALIZED MEMORIAL CARD

Though I had never seen a personalized memorial card, I knew the standardized cards provided by funeral directors were not what we would use. This was our alternative, which can be printed on a copy machine.

Sample memorial cards are included. Samples 1 and 2 were done on ivory bond or copy-machine-weight paper folded to card size. This works well if one wishes to use 4 1/2" x 5 3/4" matching envelopes. A memorial card was included in each thank-you note and holiday card (see page 254). The third and fourth samples on pages 241 and 242 were run on 8 1/2 " x 11" card stock.

Step 1:   Select materials to be included:
- Picture
- Poem
- Birth and death dates and places
- Memorial organization address
- Artwork
- Map to after-service gathering
- Words to songs (remember acknowledgment)

Step 2:   Design, lay out, paste up and take camera-ready art to printer or copy center. It may be easiest to call a graphic artist unless you have the necessary equipment and skills. Designers are usually listed under "Graphics" in the telephone book's Yellow Pages.

Step 3:   Explain what you need and the time schedule to the graphic artist on the phone. Make an appointment. Ask for a written cost estimate for the job. If the card is no more involved than the examples shown in this section, the cost will likely be minimal.

Step 4:   Take the following to the appointment:
- Selected materials from Step 1
- List of questions
    - Design questions
    - When will the job be completed?
    - May I have a written estimate of costs?

Step 5:   Call the artist at the appointed completion time. Before taking your job to the printer or copy center, check it very carefully. Have someone besides you proofread it.

Step 6:   Be sure the printer or copy machine operator gives you a written cost estimate, as well as a delivery time, at least twelve hours prior to time of service.

Sample 1
Cover

Sample 1
Inside

A Child is Loaned

"I'll lend you for a little time a child of mine, He said. It may be months, thirteen years, thirty five or ninety three. Will you, till I call him back, take care of him for me? His charms will gladden you. He'll bring frustrations that will help you grow. Yet, his stay will seem far too brief, and you'll have memories as solace for your grief. I cannot promise he will stay, since all from earth go on. But there are lessons taught down there I want this child to learn. I've looked this wide world over in my search for teachers true and from the throngs that crowd life's lanes, I have selected you."

"Now, will you give him all your love nor think the labor vain. Nor hate Me when I call his flight and take him back again?"

"I think that I heard us answer God. 'Dear Lord, thy will be done.' For all the joy Thy child shall bring the risk of grief we'll run. We'll shelter him with tenderness. We'll love him while we may. For all the happiness we've known, forever grateful stay. Should his flight be called much sooner than we've planned. We'll brave the bitter grief that comes and try to understand."

Author Unknown

IN MEMORY OF

DEREK ANDREW DAVIES

BORN

FEBRUARY 5, 1971

OXNARD, CALIFORNIA

DIED

AUGUST 24, 1984

SAN LUIS OBISPO, CALIFORNIA

MEMORIAL SERVICE

AUGUST 29, 1984

11:00 A.M.

UNITED METHODIST CHURCH

SAN LUIS OBISPO

See acknowledgment on page 268.

Sample 1
Opened Out

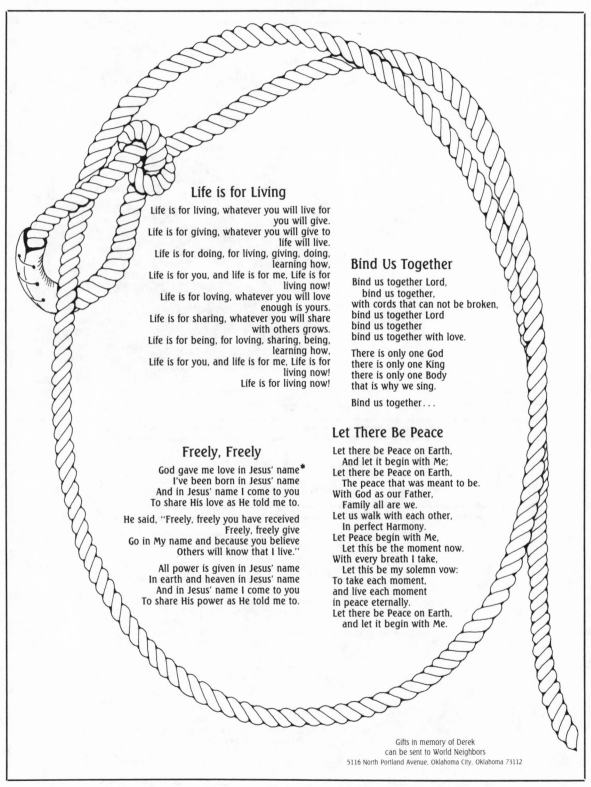

Life is for Living

Life is for living, whatever you will live for
you will give.
Life is for giving, whatever you will give to
life will live.
Life is for doing, for living, giving, doing,
learning how,
Life is for you, and life is for me, Life is for
living now!
Life is for loving, whatever you will love
enough is yours.
Life is for sharing, whatever you will share
with others grows.
Life is for being, for loving, sharing, being,
learning how,
Life is for you, and life is for me, Life is for
living now!
Life is for living now!

Bind Us Together

Bind us together Lord,
  bind us together,
with cords that can not be broken,
bind us together Lord
bind us together
bind us together with love.

There is only one God
there is only one King
there is only one Body
that is why we sing.

Bind us together...

Freely, Freely

God gave me love in Jesus' name*
I've been born in Jesus' name
And in Jesus' name I come to you
To share His love as He told me to.

He said, "Freely, freely you have received
Freely, freely give
Go in My name and because you believe
Others will know that I live."

All power is given in Jesus' name
In earth and heaven in Jesus' name
And in Jesus' name I come to you
To share His power as He told me to.

Let There Be Peace

Let there be Peace on Earth,
  And let it begin with Me;
Let there be Peace on Earth,
  The peace that was meant to be.
With God as our Father,
  Family all are we.
Let us walk with each other,
  In perfect Harmony.
Let Peace begin with Me,
  Let this be the moment now.
With every breath I take,
  Let this be my solemn vow:
To take each moment,
and live each moment
in peace eternally.
Let there be Peace on Earth,
  and let it begin with Me.

Gifts in memory of Derek
can be sent to World Neighbors
5116 North Portland Avenue. Oklahoma City, Oklahoma 73112

See acknowledgment on page 268.

Photo courtesy of Times Press Recorder

Inside

VJ Joe Vieira VJ
1916 - 1986

On May 17, 1986, Daddy passed away quietly at home in his sleep. No pain, no illness, just everlasting peace. He never feared death because he was so happy with life.

Simple things gave him pleasure. Small talk in the morning over coffee with "The Boys." A drive up the coast with friends. Watching the vegetables grow in the garden, or the honeysuckle creep up the vines.

He always enjoyed a party. Everyone was welcome at his table, either for dinner or a friendly game of cards; he wasn't particular. His clever sense of humor made everyone feel at home.

He loved a good parade, waving at his friends from atop his horse. He was most at home on horseback. A neighbor's roundup or friendly ride, it didn't matter. Retirement for Daddy was an excuse to ride his horses.

His sudden passing has left a great void in our lives. We will miss him deeply. But for all the pain we feel, it is made bearable because of our dear friends.

We can never express our gratitude to all of you. The friendship and caring, special acts of kindness and words of comfort. The many gifts of flowers and food, cards and Masses. Each embrace, every prayer have made us that much stronger and so very proud to be his family. We are very lucky to have had such a man for a husband, father and friend, and when it was time to say good-bye, we had all of you to help.

Mary, Mechell, Dale, Mark, Mike, Martha, Mitch, Rosalind

See acknowledgment on page 268.

Sample 3
Cover

Inside

All the lives going along together every life is a full life and it completed every moment it is completed

i carry your heart with me (i carry it in
my heart)
i am never without it (anywhere
i go you go,
my dear; and whatever is done
by only me is your doing, my darling)

                        i fear

no fate (for you are my fate, my sweet) i want
no world (for beautiful you are my world, my true)
and it's you are whatever a moon has always meant
and whatever a sun will always sing is you

here is the deepest secret nobody knows
(here is the root of the root and the bud of the bud
and the sky of the sky of a tree called life; which grows
higher than soul can hope or mind can hide)
and this is the wonder that's keeping the stars apart

i carry your heart (i carry it in my heart)
                    e.e. cummings

In memory of
Brett Damon Gillespie

Born
November 3, 1970

Died
January 29, 1986

Memorial Service
February 3, 1986
3:30 p.m.
United Methodist Church
San Luis Obispo

or finished or over every moment it begins all over again. We are.

We live. We love. Across a void of mystery and dread bid the tender light of faith to share.

See acknowledgment on page 268.

TO EACH, A SEASON

*The quality of a life . . . the richness
of its minutes . . . is all that really matters.
Only those moments touched by care, effort, joy
and love are of lasting value.*

*There is a special quality to the hours we pass
with those we care for. Like the light
of dusk, it lingers long after the
moment itself is gone. Those
who have become dear to us
should never be denied the
knowledge of how deeply they
have touched our lives.*
---*Robert Sexton*

We love you "Mr. Mark"!

Please join us in continuing Mark's search for answers.
Contributions may be sent to:
Cancer Research Institute - Bone Marrow Transplant
Dr. Marek Bozdech, Director
University of California at San Francisco
505 Parnassus Avenue
San Francisco, California 94143

We wish to thank all those people who generously responded to
Mark's needs with blood and platelets, and with their prayers, cards, visits,
letters and phone calls. Your response and support made an immeasurable
difference to Mark and to us.

A Time To Remember

MARK CHRISTOPHER KARNER
1965-1987

A Time To Remember
MARK CHRISTOPHER KARNER

Birthdate:	April 16, 1965
Birthplace:	Concord, Mass.
Date of death:	July 5, 1987
Place of death:	San Francisco, CA
Officiating:	Those who loved him

In the course of 65 days in the hospital, as Mark
watched his body change, he couldn't help but wonder if
that changed who he was. During the past week, friends
and family re affirmed to him the Mark they knew. We
placed a large sheet of paper on the wall at the foot of his
bed. Each person who came to see him wrote the words
that best described Mark to them. We wrote:

MARK IS:

Sensitive	Powerful	Caring	Deserving of only good
Wonderful	Tenacious!	Gentle	A good person
Determined	Agreeable	Gutsy!	Trustworthy
Unselfish	Diplomatic	Brave	Amazing
Cooperative	Extraordinary	Clear	A good friend & brother
Generous	Creative	Patient	Playful
Integrious	Supportive	Helpful	Tenacious!
Honorable	A loving son		Calm

Do not stand on my grave and weep; I am not there. I do not
sleep. I am a thousand winds that blow. I am the diamond
glints on snow. I am the sunlight on ripened grain. I am the
gently autumn's rain. when you awaken in the morning hush,
I am the swift uplifting rush of quiet birds in circled flight. I
am the soft stars that shine at night. Do not stand at my grave
and cry; I am not there. I did not die.. —Unknown

TO ALL PARENTS

"I'll lend you for a little time a child of mine," he said.
"For you to love the while he lives, and mourn for
  when he's dead.
It may be for six or seven years, or twenty-two or
  three;
But will you, till I call him back, take care
  of him for Me?
He'll bring his charms to gladden you:
  and should his stay be brief,
You'll have his lovely memories
  as solace for your grief.

I cannot promise he will stay since
  all from earth return.
But there are lessons taught down
  there I want this child to learn.
I've looked the wide world over,
  in my search for teachers true.
And from the throngs that crowd
  life's lanes I have selected you.

Now will you give him all your love
  nor think the labor vain,
Nor hate Me when I come to call, to take him back again?"
I fancied that I heard them say, 'Dear Lord, Thy will be done,
for all the joy Thy child will bring the risk of grief we'llrun.

We'll shelter him with tenderness, we'll love him
  while we may
And for the happiness we have known forever grateful stay;
But shall the angels call him much sooner than we've
  planned, We'll brave the bitter grief that comes and
  try to understand.'" —Edgar A. Guest

See acknowledgment on page 268.

Ideas for memorial card . . .

MEMORIAL OR FUNERAL SERVICE DETAILS

The purpose of a memorial service is to help people say good-bye to a loved one in a positive way. There are important decisions in preparing for a memorial service. Tradition need not bind the experience.

BEFORE PLANNING THE SERVICE

Call the attorney holding a copy of the will. Find out the name of the executor and any upon-death instructions. In most cases, it is possible to choose whether or not — and to what degree — you wish assistance from clergy.

DATE OF SERVICE

1. Within two days after obituary notices appear in newspapers
2. Allow travel time for those coming some distance.

HOUR OF SERVICE

1. After school is out if many youths are involved
2. An 11 a.m. service may allow working people to participate more easily

PLACE OF SERVICE

1. If at a church, choose appropriate size and denomination
2. If outside a church, choose a location easy to find

MEMORIAL CARDS

1. Standard, provided by mortician
2. Personalized (see page 236)
   Consider including:
     - picture of the deceased
     - poem
     - birth and death dates and places
     - words to be sung and/or repeated at service need to have
       credit line for source
     - address of Memorial Fund (donors usually appreciate the
       privacy of donating to an institution rather than
       to a family memorial address)
     - map or address of after-service gathering

MUSIC AT SERVICE

1. Instrumental or vocal
2. Select musicians or ask for recommendations from clergy
   or mortician.
3. Specify what songs the family wishes to use. It is helpful for you
   to give musicians preference guidelines regarding the type
   of music if songs are not specified.

*Note: Be sure to mention songs or types of music that would
be unacceptable to family members.*

PARTICIPANTS AT SERVICE (any or all of these)

1. Clergy (usually appreciate family input)
2. Family
3. Friends
4. Business associates and professionals

ORDER OF SERVICE (length should not exceed 45 minutes)

1.	Music	as people arrive
2.	Opening	prayer, Scripture reading, poem, statement
3.	Singing	solo or choral
4.	Service	liturgy, remembrances by family and friends
5.	Announcement	invitation to after-service gathering, including location — or post maps at door
6.	Closing	songs, Scripture reading, poetry or prayers

INTERMENT

1. Public or private
2. By clergy and/or only by family

MISCELLANEOUS ITEMS

1. Record the service on videotape.
   (We found this a valuable
   grief tool for those unable to attend.)

2. The gathering afterward is very important.
   (For us, this launched our healing of grief.)
   - At all exits, post a map marking both service location and
     gathering location.
   - A potluck allows people to help easily.
   - Having pizzas delivered is an easy solution, especially in the
     case of teen-agers.
   - Serving only desserts or hors d'oeuvres is another option.

3. Preferences of the deceased and of family members are
   important guides in planning services.

4. Books the deceased used are usually marked or contain
   valuable memorial service material.

5. Nurses and other care-givers frequently appreciate being
   included, since a close relationship often evolves in cases
   of prolonged illness.

6. At the service a memorial record book, which includes a guest register,
   is meaningful for most families.

Memorial service ideas I want to remember . . .

MY HOLIDAY SURVIVAL CHECKLIST

How can there be "happy holidays" when one has experienced the loss of a loved one? The emptiness and dread of the winter holidays are foreboding to a grieving family. The lights, ornaments and expectations just add clutter to the confused mass of decisions, memories, guilt and anger of grief.

Recognition that this group of four holidays is approaching allows a person or a family to move through these special occasions more easily. It is important to anticipate them with some forethought.

- Thanksgiving   –   Recent death makes it hard to feel thankful about anything.

- Hanukkah   –   The focus on light increases awareness of the darkness felt in grief.

- Christmas   –   Time when families are traditionally together; the feeling of loss and loneliness can be overwhelming.

- New Year's Day –   Anticipating the year ahead is especially difficult when one is grieving.

Most other holidays — Father's Day, Mother's Day, Valentine's Day — are scattered throughout the year, unless they fall near the birthday or death anniversary. The clustering and progressiveness of the winter holidays make them particularly difficult.

All these celebrations can be pleasant and growing experiences.
Discuss your plans and feelings about the holidays with other family
members. Remember that grief is a tough climb and a draining experience.
Remind yourself that "I have to stay in low gear to make it. Let's keep
things simple."

GENERAL POINTS TO REMEMBER

1. Asking each person what one aspect or tradition makes each
   holiday special, such as:
   - creamed onions for Thanksgiving dinner
   - sending Christmas or Hanukkah cards
   - lighting Hanukkah lights
   - singing Christmas carols
   - squash pie for Christmas dinner
   - chocolate chip cookies for New Year's Day

   Build your holiday plans to include these "special" requests.

2. Remember that holidays are really found in your heart. Joy comes
   in reaching out to touch others' lives. Watch for those tiny happy
   memories in your thoughts and let them lead you in what you
   need to do.

3. Choose to do activities that bring peace and joy, not pain and chaos.

4. Choose to do a few things rather than many. Do one at a time.

5. Consider incorporating some new or old traditions. You may wish
   to recall the religious roots from which these holidays evolved.

6. Other things to do:
   - Write out your feelings about the holidays.
   - Write a holiday letter to the person you miss so much.
   - Provide quiet sharing time for immediate family.
   - Have a memory candle burning during meals.
   - Contribute to:
     - WORLD NEIGHBORS
     - Compassionate Friends
     - Hospice

Keep the holidays focused on those who are living and what is meaningful
to them. Ask family members what traditions they cherish. Decide which
are most important to you.

Look for and focus on the happy holiday memories. Also find the happy
moments of today.

A CHECKLIST HELPS ME DECIDE WHAT TO DO

Cook Thanksgiving or holiday dinner
- have a potluck at home
- attend a potluck somewhere else
  - church
  - Compassionate Friends
  - other support groups
- have a small, simple dinner at home
- have a dessert potluck
- go to a restaurant
- prepare special traditional foods
- volunteer to help with holiday dinner
  - at church
  - at "people's kitchen"

Cards
- send no holiday cards
- send a few holiday cards
- send a holiday letter

Note: *We found it easiest to send cards early, thus allowing people to respond in their own notes to us. Sign cards and address envelopes in October. Stuff them in November. Send them after Thanksgiving. I suggest using memorial cards to explain the death most easily.*

Shopping
- buy no gifts
- buy a few gifts
- buy a gift for everyone in the family
- buy something special to wear for the holidays
- select gifts for co-workers and teachers
- make gifts
- shop by mail
- do all shopping in one day, keeping it simple
- make list before shopping

Holiday baking
- cookies
- fruitcake
- homemade jams, jellies

Decorating the house
- a little
- with someone helping you
- a lot
- selected rooms
- outside your home

A tree
- buy a living tree
- cut one yourself
- buy one at a tree lot
- put one on the grave

A holiday trip
- with your family
- go see family
- alone
- with a friend
- visit someone you seldom see at any other time

"Going out" on holiday/"going out" on New Year's Day
- attending traditional religious services
- attending special activities for children
- parties
- dancing

Hang stockings
- none
- all but one
- all of the stockings
- put small gifts for visitors in the special stocking

Doing something for others
- Give a memorial gift to (WORLD NEIGHBORS) in your loved one's name.
- Give a memorial gift to (WORLD NEIGHBORS) in the name of other loved ones.
- Give a Hospice Light.
- Give a "love gift" to Compassionate Friends.

Inviting others to share your celebration
- single persons
- senior citizens
- foreign students
- out-of-state students

The author recommends obtaining a copy of:

AWAY FOR THE HOLIDAY
by Patricia Carpenter
PCA Publishing
P.O. Box 16066
Minneapolis, MN 55416
(612) 927-5270

HANDLING THE HOLIDAYS
by Bruce Conley
Thum Printing
P.O. Box A
Elburn, IL 60119
(312) 365-6414

Other holiday survival ideas . . .

OUR FIRST HOLIDAY LETTER

Cover

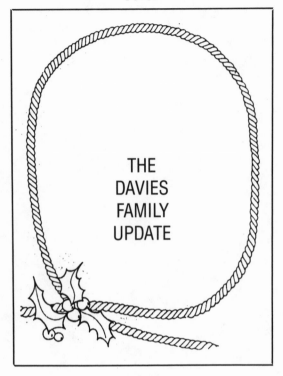

THE
DAVIES
FAMILY
UPDATE

Inside

HOLIDAY SEASON 1984

We began this unforgettable year,

with the four of us enjoying the adventure of planning what we wanted to accomplish in 1984 and during the coming five years. With a goal of investing in memories, we help the children move toward independence and developing their own abilities to contribute to improving our world.

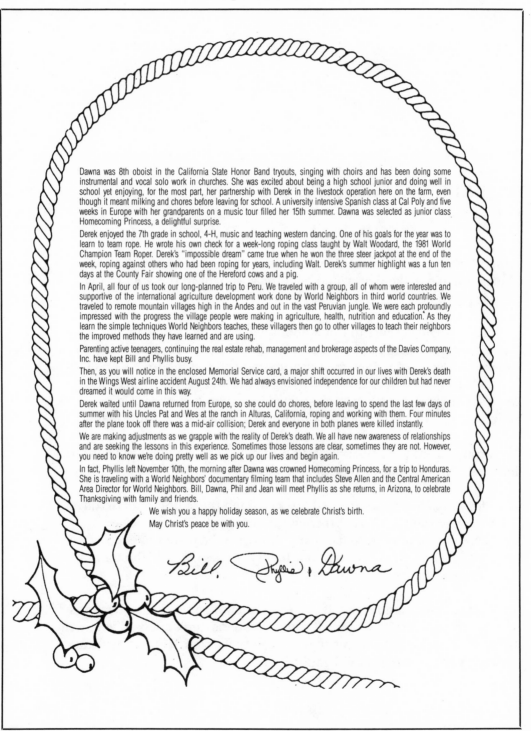

Dawna was 8th oboist in the California State Honor Band tryouts, singing with choirs and has been doing some instrumental and vocal solo work in churches. She was excited about being a high school junior and doing well in school yet enjoying, for the most part, her partnership with Derek in the livestock operation here on the farm, even though it meant milking and chores before leaving for school. A university intensive Spanish class at Cal Poly and five weeks in Europe with her grandparents on a music tour filled her 15th summer. Dawna was selected as junior class Homecoming Princess, a delightful surprise.

Derek enjoyed the 7th grade in school, 4-H, music and teaching western dancing. One of his goals for the year was to learn to team rope. He wrote his own check for a week-long roping class taught by Walt Woodard, the 1981 World Champion Team Roper. Derek's "impossible dream" came true when he won the three steer jackpot at the end of the week, roping against others who had been roping for years, including Walt. Derek's summer highlight was a fun ten days at the County Fair showing one of the Hereford cows and a pig.

In April, all four of us took our long-planned trip to Peru. We traveled with a group, all of whom were interested and supportive of the international agriculture development work done by World Neighbors in third world countries. We traveled to remote mountain villages high in the Andes and out in the vast Peruvian jungle. We were each profoundly impressed with the progress the village people were making in agriculture, health, nutrition and education. As they learn the simple techniques World Neighbors teaches, these villagers then go to other villages to teach their neighbors the improved methods they have learned and are using.

Parenting active teenagers, continuing the real estate rehab, management and brokerage aspects of the Davies Company, Inc. have kept Bill and Phyllis busy.

Then, as you will notice in the enclosed Memorial Service card, a major shift occurred in our lives with Derek's death in the Wings West airline accident August 24th. We had always envisioned independence for our children but had never dreamed it would come in this way.

Derek waited until Dawna returned from Europe, so she could do chores, before leaving to spend the last few days of summer with his Uncles Pat and Wes at the ranch in Alturas, California, roping and working with them. Four minutes after the plane took off there was a mid-air collision; Derek and everyone in both planes were killed instantly.

We are making adjustments as we grapple with the reality of Derek's death. We all have new awareness of relationships and are seeking the lessons in this experience. Sometimes those lessons are clear, sometimes they are not. However, you need to know we're doing pretty well as we pick up our lives and begin again.

In fact, Phyllis left November 10th, the morning after Dawna was crowned Homecoming Princess, for a trip to Honduras. She is traveling with a World Neighbors' documentary filming team that includes Steve Allen and the Central American Area Director for World Neighbors. Bill, Dawna, Phil and Jean will meet Phyllis as she returns, in Arizona, to celebrate Thanksgiving with family and friends.

We wish you a happy holiday season, as we celebrate Christ's birth.

May Christ's peace be with you.

Bill, Phyllis & Dawna

EASING GRIEF FOR OTHERS

Other than a will, I had not thought about information I could gather and choices I could make that would help those caught in the grief process after my own death.

I am encouraging others to think about choices that can be made. These choices can be made at any time, then re-evaluated annually. They are worth discussing. Even as a death approaches, the discussion of these points is frequently a relief to the dying individual. If necessary, one designated family member or close friend can slowly gather this information, by asking one question on each visit during conversation.

Pre-arrangement (of the service and burial details) is a great relief for most families. The fees may also be paid in advance.

Use this guide to help your loved ones through those first difficult days after you are gone. It will tell them what you want. How you want it. Where your important papers are. And give them step-by-step instructions and other information that will make many of the inevitable early decisions a lot easier to make.

Fill in this guide completely. If you can't answer some of the questions at first, go back to them later. If some questions don't apply to you, write "N/A" (Not Applicable). You can ask a mortuary counselor for assistance, usually with no charge or obligation.

See acknowledgment on page 268.

256

When you've completed this information, tell your family members where they can find the original and give several relatives a copy. It is also a good idea to leave a copy with your attorney and the mortuary.

This information and these instructions DO NOT CONSTITUTE A WILL.

LETTER OF INSTRUCTION

In an effort to help in closing my affairs, I have compiled this letter of instruction as a guide. This document should not be confused with my will. It cannot provide for the testamentary disposition of property, which can be accomplished only with a will.

SPECIFIC FUNERAL, MEMORIAL AND BURIAL INSTRUCTIONS

1. These are my burial instructions:

    [ ] Funeral Service   [ ] Interment

    [ ] Memorial Service   [ ] Burial

    [ ] No Service   [ ] Cremation

    [ ] Religious Service   [ ] Scattering of Ashes

    [ ] Graveside Service   [ ] Location:

    [ ] Fraternal Service   [ ] Other Service:

2. I have made arrangements with:

    Name of facility:

    Address:

    City/State/Zip:

    Phone: ( )   Contact Person:

3. I have purchased a burial plot at:

    Address:

    City/State/Zip:

    Phone: ( )   Contact Person:

4. I would like this person to officiate at the service:

                         Name   Phone (   )

    [ ] Clergy

    [ ] Family member(s)

    [ ] Friend(s)

5. I would like these people to serve as pallbearers:

    Name   Phone (   )

6. I prefer

    [ ] Flowers

    [ ] Donations be made in my name to these organizations:

    Name   Address   City/State/Zip   Phone

7. I prefer

    [ ] Taped music of this type:

    [ ] Live music: Organist/Pianist   Soloist   Other:

    Specific songs:

8. I would like to be dressed in this clothing:

9. This is information you'll need for my burial permit and obituary notices:

ABOUT ME

    • My full, legal name:

    • My nickname:

- My religion:

- My occupation and title:

    Employer:

    Type of business:

    Previous employers:

- Previous occupations/businesses:

- My Social Security number:

- I attended these schools/colleges and earned these degrees:

- Honors, scholarships and awards I earned in school include:

- I am a member of these organizations:

    Organization   Leadership Position

- I have held these public, charitable, civic or religious offices:

- I have received these awards or honors:

- I am particularly proud of these accomplishments:

- I served in this branch of the military:

    From (date)   Until (date)   Rank

- I received these military honors:

- Service papers' number:

- My hobbies or special interests:

- Other accomplishments:

ABOUT MY FAMILY

My spouse's name:

My children:

Name	Address	City/State/Zip	Phone	D.O.B.

I was married: Date   Location

My maiden name:

My father's name:

My father's birthplace:

My mother's name:

My mother's birthplace:

My brother(s) name(s):

My sister(s) name(s):

I was separated/divorced:

My former spouse's name:

Famous family members:

My family's ethnic origins:

Facts and dates of historical significance in my family:

Please also include this information in my obituary notices:

10. These are the eulogy materials, poems, stories or meaningful
    Scripture I like that might be included in a memorial service:

IMPORTANT DOCUMENTS
AND PROFESSIONAL COUNSELORS

1. These are places where you will find my important documents:

    Current will:

    Trust documents:

    Insurance policies (do not keep policies in bank safe-deposit box):

    Auto:

    Home:

    Health:

    Life:

    Other:

    Bank accounts: Bank Name/Location   Account Number

    Stocks, bonds, other securities:

    List of investments:

    Deeds and mortgages:

    Last three years' tax returns:

    Current financial statements:

    This year's financial records:

    Credit cards and numbers:

List of debts and contract payments:

Employment or partnership agreements:

Military discharge papers:

Social Security papers:

Driver's license:

Birth certificate:

Marriage license:

Citizenship papers:

Safe location: Combination/Key:

Safe-deposit box location:
                     Number: Key Location:

House keys:

Other:

2. These are the professionals upon whom I have relied for counsel:

My attorney:

   Address:

   City/State/Zip:

   Phone: (   )

My accountant:

   Address:

   City/State/Zip:

   Phone: (   )

My physician:

   Address:

   City/State/Zip:

   Phone: (   )

My insurance agent:

    Address:

    City/State/Zip:

    Phone: (   )

My stockbroker or investment counselor:

    Address:

    City/State/Zip:

    Phone: (   )

Other:

REQUESTS TO THE CORONER, MORTICIAN OR OTHERS

In addition, some requests can lessen the grief trauma for the survivors. These requests may be made through Hospice or another organization if you are unable or unsuccessful in making them personally. Insist that the request *ALWAYS* be made in writing, and includes signatures and also be dated.

1. The black bag is to be zipped or the sheet is to cover the face of the deceased *after* being placed in the vehicle rather than done inside the home or in the presence of family members.

2. Family members may request that they be allowed to assist in the preparation of the body at the mortuary.

3. An autopsy is either not to be made unless it is mandatory or be made regardless of circumstances.

4. Specify and note on driver's license which body parts, if any, are to be donated for transplant or research and designate to which organization or institution. Hospice and other organizations may be helpful in making arrangements.

Note: Accepting institutions usually require that arrangements be made IN WRITING and IN ADVANCE of a death. This is usually a comforting decision for both the dying person and for survivors.

5. Additional requests:

LIFE-SUPPORT SYSTEMS INSTRUCTION

A Living Will is a document that allows you to instruct your physicians, family and attorney not to use artificial means to extend your life. This is to be done only when there is no expectation of recovery and when such methods will interrupt the natural death process. It permits you to have a choice in the ultimate decision about the continuance of your life. It also should specifically mention the fact that you do not wish cardiopulmonary resuscitation (CPR) and feeding tubes to be used, if that is your wish.

Living Wills are not legal in all states. An attorney, physician, medical association and local Hospice chapters are among those who can explain the laws that pertain to the state where you reside. In California, for example, a state law requires completion of a form called *"Durable Power of Attorney for Health Care."* This document allows the selection of another person who can make health care decisions for you when you are unable to do so yourself. The forms are readily obtainable from stationery stores, physicians or the California Medical Association. The Society for the Right to Die is a national organization dedicated to assisting individuals wishing to express this intention. (Address and phone number are on page 266). Even though it may not be legally binding, a Living Will expresses your desires, and it serves as a guideline for your family and physicians. *WRITE* your wishes clearly, *DATE* and *SIGN* the document, and discuss the matter with those who will be responsible for making decisions about your health care.

Have your Living Will witnessed by two persons who are unrelated to you by blood or marriage; these persons should not be your future care-providers and should not be mentioned in your will. It is wise to review your Living Will at regular intervals; date and initial any change or addition.

Keep the original and updated copies of this vital document where they can readily be found and provide updated copies to appropriate persons. An identification card with these instructions should be in your wallet.

Note: *Legal forms for California residents are available in most stationery stores.* **This is not a legal document.**

MY LIVING WILL

TO ALL WHOM IT MAY CONCERN,

especially

MY FAMILY, MY PHYSICIANS AND MY ATTORNEY:

I realize this is not an official legal document and that it will not be recognized in all states or nations, yet I, _____, being of sound mind, do herein express my strong, carefully considered desires in the event that physical or mental disability should prevent me from making decisions regarding the prolonging of my life by artificial means.

I recognize that death is part of the continuum of the birth, maturing and aging process, and so I do not fear it. Therefore, I avidly request that if there is no expectation whatsoever for my recovery, I be allowed to die naturally and peacefully and not unduly kept alive by artificial means, including medication, feeding tubes or cardiopulmonary resuscitation (CPR). I would hope, however, that any medications that would relieve my suffering might be given, even though they might shorten the remainder of my life.

Insofar as this document may not legally be enforceable, I urge that those to whom I entrust my welfare in this matter consider the directions herein set forth to be morally binding.

Signature _____ Date _____

Witness _____ Date _____

Witness _____ Date _____

Copies of this request have been given to my physicians, close friends and relatives, whose names, addresses and phone numbers are listed:

HELPFUL ORGANIZATIONS

Call national offices for local contacts in your area.

Hospice is a national organization with over 1,200 local branches that provide a wide range of assistance both prior to and after a death.

National Hospice Organization   (800) 331-1620
1901 N. Fort Myer – 407   (703) 243-5900
Arlington, VA 22209

Compassionate Friends is a national organization for — and of — families experiencing the death of a child. They have many local chapters.

Compassionate Friends   (312) 990-0010
P.O. Box 3696   after 11/11/89
Oak Brook, IL 60522-3696   (708) 990-0010

The Society for the Right To Die is a national organization that will provide free information and forms for a Living Will that are acceptable in the state where you reside. Maintains counseling and legal referral service.

Society for the Right To Die   (212) 246-6973
250 West 57th Street
New York, NY 10107

Medical associations in most states will provide Living Will information or direct you to a source. Check for specific documents authorized by individual state laws. The California Medical Association will provide information regarding a Living Will and life-support systems releases. They also have a list of other state medical associations.

California Medical Association   (415) 863-5522
P.O. Box 7690
San Francisco, CA 94102-7690

Other support organizations with which we have had contact:

Children's Hospice International   (703) 684-0330
1101 King Street, Suite 131   (800) 2-4-CHILD
Alexandria, VA 22314

Parents of Murdered Children   (513) 721-5683
100 E. Eighth Street B-41
Cincinnati, OH 45202

Candlelighters Childhood Cancer Foundation   (202) 659-5136
Suite 1011, 1901 Pennsylvania Ave., N.W.
Washington, D.C. 20006

California Sudden Infant Death Syndrome Project   (415) 540-2111
2151 Berkeley Way, Annex 4
Berkeley, CA 94704

Catholic Service League   (216) 788-8726
5385 Market Street
Youngstown, OH 44512

Hope For Bereaved   (315) 472-HOPE
Support Groups and Services   (472-4673)
1342 Lancaster Avenue
Syracuse, NY 13210

The Jewish Community Hospice   (301) 881-3700 ext. 940
(A program of the Jewish Social Service Agency)
6123 Montrose Road
Rockville, MD 20852

Survivors of Suicide   (414) 437-7527
630 Greene Avenue
Green Bay, WI 54301

Widowed Persons Association of California Inc.   (916) 972-WPAC
State Office P.O. Box 60619
Sacramento, CA 95860-0619

Cope   (614) 369-8420
(A support group for grieving parents)
425 Senate Avenue
Delaware, OH 43015

Empty Arms   (814) 838-6346
6416 Wyndham Court
Erie, PA 16505

H.E.A.R.T.   (313) 532-0712
(Helping Empty Arms Reach For Tomorrow)
12883 Wormer
Redford, MI 48239

ACKNOWLEDGMENTS

Grateful acknowledgment is made to the following for permission to reprint previously published materials:

Page   31 *Untitled Poem* by Karl Kempton.

66 *The Seed* by Dawna Davies.

178 *You'll Never Walk Alone* by Richard Rodgers and Oscar Hammerstein II. © 1945 Williamson Music, Inc. Copyright renewed. Sole selling agent, T.B. Harns Company (c/o The Welk Music Group, Santa Monica, CA 90401) International copyright secured. All rights reserved. Used by permission.

180, 242, 238
A Child Is Loaned in variation appears to be *To All Parents* by Edgar Guest, though original source noted, as author unknown. *To All Parents* from *"All In A Lifetime"* by Edgar Guest © 1938. reprinted by permission of Ayer Company Publications, Salem, NH.

196, 239
Life Is for Living © 1967. Words and music by Carmen Moshier. Used by permission.

197, 239
Freely, Freely © 1972 by Lexicon Music, Inc. ASCAP. All rights reserved. International copyright secured. Used by special permission. Originally, *God forgave my sins in Jesus' name.

198, 239
Bind Us Together. Words and music by Bob Gillman. © 1977 by Thank You Music, U.K. All rights reserved. Used by permission. Administered in the United States by Gaither Music Company.

199, 239
Let There Be Peace, Let There Be Peace on Earth © 1955 by Jan-Lee Music. Words by Jill Jackson. Used by special permission.

200 Telegram-Tribune, San Luis Obispo, California.

201 Dunsmuir News. Dunsmuir, California.

216 Developed with the help of Sutcliff Lawn Memorial Mortuary, Reis Chapels and other local mortuaries.

240 Mary Vieira.

240 Times Press Recorder, Grover City, California

241 Val and Sandy Gillespie.

241 Copyright 1952 by E.E. Cummings. Reprinted from his volume Complete Poems 1913-1962 by permission of Harcourt, Brace Jovanovich, Inc.

242 Gary and Pandora Nash-Karner.

242 Copyright 1985 by Robert Sexton. Reprinted from his volume An American Romantic by Robert Sexton, 491 Greenwich St., San Francisco, CA 94610

256 Co-developed by Los Osos Valley Memorial Park and Mortuary, and Pandora Nash-Karner of Pandora and Co. together with Phyllis Davies.

BOOKS THE AUTHOR FOUND HELPFUL

The authors of the following books have gently taken my hand and walked with me along my path of grief. Although grief is an individual experience, you may also find these books helpful.

The Bible	
Accept This Gift	Francis Vaughan
The Courage To Grieve	Judy Tatelbaum
Writing the Natural Way	Gabriele Rico
The Bereaved Parent	Harriet Sarnoff Schiff
A Course in Miracles	Foundation for Inner Peace
The Prophet	Kahlil Gibran
Love Is Letting Go of Fear	Gerald Jampolsky
Teach Only Love	Gerald Jampolsky
Good-bye to Guilt	Gerald Jampolsky
I, Monty	Marcus Bach
Illusions	Richard Bach
Good Grief	Granger Westberg
A Man's Reach	Glenn Clark
Soul Sincere Desire	Glenn Clark
Channels of Spiritual Power	Frank Laubach
Life After Loss	Bob Deitz

BOOKS ON GRIEF RECOMMENDED TO THE AUTHOR

I Never Know What To Say	Nina Herrmann Donnelley
On Death and Dying	Elisabeth Kübler-Ross
Don't Take My Grief Away From Me	Doug Manning
My Son... My Son	Iris Bolton
When Bad Things Happen to Good People	Harold S. Kushner
When a Baby Dies	Sara Wheeler and Rana Limbo
Necessary Losses	Judith Viorst
How To Survive the Loss of a Love	Colgrove, Bloomfield, Williams
Who Dies?	Steven Levine
Healing into Living and Dying	Steven Levine
Remember the Secret	Elisabeth Kübler-Ross
Men Who Have Walked With God	Sheldon Cheney
A Grief Observed	C.S. Lewis
The Secret Garden	Frances Hodgson Burnett
Mister God, This Is Anna	Fynn
When Someone You Love Has AIDS	Betty-Clair Moffatt
Stepping Stones to Grief Recovery	Deborah Roth
No Time For Good-byes	Janice Harris Lord
Life is Good-bye – Life is Hello	Alla Bozarth-Campbell

If you have found this book helpful, you may
wish to suggest it to someone else or obtain a copy
for a friend in need.

LYLE STUART INC.
120 Enterprise Avenue
Secaucus, New Jersey 07094

For autographed or dedicated books please write:

Phyllis Davies • P.O. Box 945 • San Luis Obispo, CA 93406